D1242394

THE KEATS
INHERITANCE

Other Books by Robert Gittings

Literary Criticism

John Keats: The Living Year
The Mask of Keats
Shakespeare's Rival
The Living Shakespeare (editor)

Plays and Poems

The Makers of Violence
Out of this Wood
Wentworth Place
Famous Meeting
This Tower My Prison

The Keats Inheritance

by

ROBERT GITTINGS

BARNES & NOBLE, Inc.

NEW YORK

PUBLISHERS & BOOKSELLERS SINCE 1873

Printed in Great Britain

Contents

Author's Note

DURING the opening stages of work on a new biography of John Keats, based far more closely than usual on original documentary sources, I became aware that there was one considerable area which had been neither explained nor fully explored in previous biographies. This was the problem of Keats's poverty—how a young man who had been well provided for in two wills, his grandfather's and his grandmother's, should find himself literally penniless before he was twenty-five, and die at that age in debt to friends and to publishers. The special importance that this lack of money assumed in his great creative year made the problem not merely academic but intimately connected with his poetry.

All his inheritance, I knew, had once been in Chancery, a name daunting to research; but clearly only by consulting the original Chancery records could anything resembling the truth be reached. Fortunately I was afforded a rare opportunity to do this by the generosity of the Phoenix Trust. Their award had bought me time to begin the main biography, and this supplementary study may be regarded as its first-fruits. I am therefore entirely and gratefully indebted to the Trust for the chance to present this work.

My indebtedness to my major source of information, the Public Record Office, is specially detailed on page 5. I must also thank those who have made the Ralph Thomas Ms. at Keats House, Hampstead so readily accessible to me, particularly the Chief Librarian and Curator, Mr William R. Maidment, and the Assistant Curator, Miss Charlotte R. Lutyens. The text of several pages of this Ms., forming Appendix VII of this book, and the facsimile of one page, used on the jacket, are published and reproduced by permission of the Public Libraries Committee of the Hampstead Borough Council. as is the short documentary extract forming Appendix VI.

The difficult area of early nineteenth-century Chancery procedure has been made clear to me by the Master Heward, who has patiently corrected or prevented many errors in interpretation, though I must absolve him from any responsibility for those I may have allowed to remain. He has also generously put at my disposal his unpublished dissertation *Causes of Delay and Expense in the Court of Chancery in the early 19th Century*. Other legal advice has been generously and helpfully given by my friends Christopher Baily and Nicolas Browne-Wilkinson. My calculations regarding the values of stock have been confirmed by a leading firm of brokers, for whose professional assistance I am extremely grateful. Among many who have helped me over matters of detail, I am especially indebted to my wife, not only for her specialized knowledge of medical history but for her general and constructive encouragement throughout.

R. G.

List of Abbreviations
for sources used in this book

A. MANUSCRIPT

F.K.L.: Correspondence between Fanny Keats Llanos and H. Buxton Forman, Keats House Collection, uncatalogued.

G.L.: Corporation of London, Guildhall Library.

P.P.R.: Principal Probate Registry, Somerset House.

P.R.O.: Public Record Office, Chancery Lane.

Ralph Thomas Ms: Transcripts etc. relating to the Keats finances, made by Ralph Thomas for Sidney Colvin, c. 1885–86, Keats House Collection, uncatalogued.

B. PRINTED

G.M.: *Gentleman's Magazine.*

KC: *The Keats Circle: Letters and Papers 1816–1879*, ed. Hyder Edward Rollins, 2 vols. 1948.

KSMB: *Keats-Shelley Memorial Bulletin.*

KSR: 'Keats's Sailor Relation', Robert Gittings, *TLS*, 15 April 1960.

Letters: *The Letters of John Keats*, ed. Hyder Edward Rollins, 2 vols. 1958.

MKO: 'Mr Keats's Origin', Robert Gittings, *TLS*, 5 March 1964.

MLPKC: *More Letters and Poems of the Keats Circle*, ed. Hyder Edward Rollins, 1955.

TLS: *The Times Literary Supplement.*

Vesey: *Reports of Cases . . . in the High Court of Chancery . . . 1789 to 1817*, Francis Vesey, Jr., 1828.

C. BIOGRAPHIES OF KEATS

Colvin: *Keats*, Sidney Colvin, 1887.

Lowell: *John Keats*, Amy Lowell, 2 vols. 1925.

Hewlett: *A Life of John Keats*, Dorothy Hewlett, 2nd ed., 1949.

Ward: *John Keats: The Making of a Poet*, Aileen Ward, 1963.

Bate: *John Keats*, Walter Jackson Bate, 1963.

Prologue

THIS book does not deal with the small but by no means negligible estate (under £2000) possessed by the poet's father when he died intestate after an accident in 1804, and of which his widow Frances obtained administration in May 1805. What happened to it after that has been the subject of some conjecture but no certainty, except that John Keats got none of it.

This is, however, the first attempt at a detailed and accurate examination of the much larger estate left by the poet's maternal grandfather, John Jennings, in which Keats had a very considerable interest. This inheritance was, or could have been, of supreme importance to a poet who never, so far as one can tell, undertook any form of paid employment during his short life. Needs and anxieties about money almost certainly hastened his breakdown in health, and became obsessive in his letters and even in his private jottings; the need to go to the Bank was 'worse than any thing in Dante',[1] and a marginal note in his copy of Burton's *The Anatomy of Melancholy* comments 'precious stones are certainly a remedy against Melancholy: a valuable diamond would effectually cure mine'.

Any biographer of Keats is faced at the outset with some curious contradictions in this story of financial worry which pervades his letters from the spring of 1817 onwards, that is from the time when he finally gave up the profession of surgery and cast his lot for poetry. One odd fact is that Keats was not by any means born in poverty, and Leigh Hunt's tactless suggestion that he was brought angry corrections from Keats's relatives and friends. Nor did he live as if he were poor. He spent money freely, lent it generously, and the impression he gave to acquaintances was evidently one of affluence. In the

[1] *Letters*, II, p. 32.

I

summer of 1817, a time when Keats had twice to write embarrassed begging letters to his publisher, Shelley, who had seen him frequently during the previous winter, advised Leigh Hunt, 'I should imagine among your intimate friends nothing could be more easy than to arrange a loan. . . . Your Brother I do not doubt will or can do nothing. But there is Keats, who certainly *can*'.[1] His later friends never seemed to question that he had private means enough to live without working at a profession, even at a time when he himself is protesting his poverty; nor even then, in 1819, does he himself appear whole-hearted in his resolve to earn money as a ship's surgeon or as a journalist. One of the most important things in Keats's life, for us, is that he habitually behaved as if he had great expectations, and so kept his mind and his life free and uninterrupted for great poetry.

Yet in spite of its importance there has probably been more misconception and factual error about this element in Keats's life than over any other. This started almost directly after his death; the quarrels among his friends, to which we owe the virtual disaster that there is no proper biography by a contemporary, were almost all due, directly or not, to varied views about Keats's money matters. Yet the chief mistake that has bedevilled modern biography dates back just 80 years. In 1885 Sidney Colvin was preparing his life of Keats for the English Men of Letters series. Colvin, although Fellow of Trinity College, Cambridge, and Slade Professor of Fine Art, was a literary amateur. He was not in the habit of doing his own research, but of asking friends and correspondents to help him, as can be seen in many notes and letters now in the Keats House Collection, Hampstead. He employed a lawyer, Ralph Thomas of 27 Chancery Lane, to look into the Chancery suit of which John Jennings's will was the subject. Thomas set about his work conscientiously, but he soon found the task of examining the Chancery documents in the Public Record Office an immense one; 'most voluminous', he commented.[2] Much of his time was wasted initially because the proceedings had been wrongly indexed by a clerk under 'Midgley', the unusual Christian name of John Jennings's

---

[1] *The Letters of Percy Bysshe Shelley*, ed. F. L. Jones, I, p. 550.
[2] Ralph Thomas Ms.

son; the correction in Thomas's hand can be seen today. There were other handicaps. 'Two days I was unable to see at the Record Office, it being so dark and they having no artificial light.' Even when he could see, Thomas found how laborious research among Chancery documents can be. 'One has to search for the proceedings and when one gets it there may be nothing in the Order or Report though it may have taken an hour or more to get.' He found he could not give more than an hour or two a day to it, and so 'I shall try to limit myself to giving you the facts you ask for'. This naturally reduced the scope and value of his enquiries, for Colvin was primarily questioning him for specific biographical points. Yet Thomas produced a notable haul of Ms. notes, which are now in the Keats House Collection. They have a number of inaccuracies—bad light, eye strain and tiredness may be detected in these—but on the purely financial side he is exhaustive and nearly complete. In February 1886 he finished triumphantly, 'I think I have now accounted for every penny of the funds herein even to finding that there is twopence more than there ought to be in Court and how it arises'. Within his set limits, he had provided material for a fairly accurate account of the basic finances of the affair.[1]

Unfortunately Colvin, not having done the work himself, and not perhaps having much aptitude for law or finance, was completely fogged by Thomas's findings. His further questions, gummed into Thomas's notes, demonstrate this; often he has not grasped the basic terms. 'Who is the "testator"?' he asks. 'John Jennings,' replies Thomas patiently. In the preface to his *Keats* in 1887, he paid a friendly tribute to Thomas, but apart from three notes in the Appendix the book contained almost nothing of the latter's work. Colvin moreover introduced something that seems to have been a pure invention of his own, and which has set every biographer since himself on the wrong track. In his Preface, he referred to Thomas's investigations in the following way:

> When Keats's maternal grandfather, Mr John Jennings, died in 1805, leaving property exceeding the amount of the specific bequests under his will, it was thought necessary that his estate should be administered by the Court of Chancery, and with

[1] Ralph Thomas Ms.

that intent a friendly suit was brought in the names of his daughter and her second husband (Frances Jennings, *m.* 1st Thomas Keats, and 2nd William Rawlings) against her mother and brother, who were the executors.

There is absolutely nothing in all the notes that Ralph Thomas sent Colvin that can justify such a description. The most misleading thing about it, the term 'friendly suit', is never used by Thomas, and seems to be a figment of Colvin's imagination.

Yet for eighty years this description has been accepted by all biographers, some of whom have added a further misconception. In a printed law series, Francis Vesey, Jr. *Reports of Cases . . . in the High Court of Chancery . . . 1789 to 1817*, a hearing and judgment in the case, dated 1806, is given. This has been treated as if it were the *beginning* of the whole case,[1] which in fact had started over a year earlier, and whose most important biographical documents are all dated 1805.[2] This strange mistake, almost as strange as Colvin's fiction of the 'friendly suit', has been combined with an arbitrary use of fragments of Thomas's notes, sometimes without acknowledgement, to produce a hotch-potch of error which has by now successfully obscured almost every trace of the original truth. The statement of the Keats inheritance offered by his biographers has become far more confusing than even the long Chancery case about it which lasted for twenty years, and outlived the poet.

Where many good and conscientious biographers of Keats have met almost total failure, it would seem rash and presumptious to claim that even partial success can be achieved. Yet there was always at hand a possible method, laborious though it was, yet worth the trouble. This was simply to refer back to the original notes by Thomas, and then, using these as rough guide, to go through the various documents—proceedings, affidavits, reports, certificates and orders in Chancery —relating to the case in the Public Record Office far more fully than he himself was able to do. Moreover, there are now facilities which he did not enjoy: not only artificial light and angle-poise lamps, quick copying and photostat reproduction,

[1] The mistake seems to originate with Lowell, I, p. 26, followed particularly by Hewlett, Appendix I, pp. 375–377, and Bate, Appendix III, pp. 705–712.

[2] See Appendices I to IV, which reproduce many of these in full.

but the courtesy, help and informed advice of the officers and Search Room staff, for which I should like to record my considerable gratitude. Although they are not Crown copyright, I should like to acknowledge the fact that some of the documents I was thus enabled to study are reproduced in full as appendices to this book, and in verbatim extract throughout the text.

With all this first-hand information, not possessed by any previous biographer of the poet, we may reassess the whole story of the Keats inheritance from its starting-point, the will of his maternal grandfather, John Jennings.

John Jennings's Will

JOHN JENNINGS, Keats's grandfather, appears to have been baptized at the City Church always associated with his name, St. Stephen, Coleman Street, and his sister Mary in the neighbouring parish of St Botolph Without, Bishopsgate. It was in this latter parish that she made her two marriages, first to Richard Havers and then to a prosperous victualler named Charles Sweetingburgh; it is as Mary Sweetingburgh that she appears in her brother's will, in which her three children, Charles, Betsy and Sarah are also mentioned.

John Jennings himself was a victualler, and he too prospered at the trade, for by the beginning of 1774 he was able to buy a leasehold property of some value, the Swan and Hoop public house and livery stables, No. 24 The Pavement, Moorgate. Just over ten years later, in 1785, he took over the lease of another valuable property next door, No. 23.[1] He let this at a rent which by the end of his life was bringing him in £46 a year, and it was sub-let in tenements.[2] He also took up mortgages on other people's property, and invested steadily in Government funds and East India stock.

Meanwhile he had married a Northcountry-woman, Alice Whalley, who seems to have had relatives in a neighbouring City parish. They had three children, of whom the eldest, Frances, was the mother of John Keats. One of her brothers, Thomas, died at the age of fourteen of 'a decline'—the common name for the all-too-common disease of tuberculosis; the other, Midgley John Jennings, went to sea, and after a brief career before the mast and as acting purser, obtained a commission in the Marines in 1796. He was promoted first lieutenant in 1799 and stationed at Chatham Barracks.[3] He had the

[1] Later numbered 22. See Appendix IV.
[2] MKO.   [3] KSR.

6

reputation of a hero with his young nephews, the Keats boys, to whom we must now turn.

On 9 October 1794, Frances Jennings married Thomas Keats at St George's, Hanover Square. She was under age and he can only have been just twenty-one. No relatives of either witnessed the marriage, and the bridegroom's profession is not given. Much later accounts describe him as waiter, butler, ostler or helper at his father-in-law's inn and stables, and give him a West country origin, though it seems more than probable he had City connections. The match seems, on the face of it, to have been a runaway one, and there is no certainty that the eldest son, John Keats, was born at the Swan and Hoop; he was baptized not at the nearby ward church of St Stephen, Coleman Street, but at St Botolph, Bishopsgate, where his date of birth was given as 31 October 1795. Another son, George, was born on 28 February 1797, and at Christmas 1798 the family moved to Craven Street, off the City Road, where two more boys, Thomas and Edward (who died young) were born. Their first known connection with the Swan and Hoop was at Christmas 1802.

By that time, John Jennings, now over 70, was retiring from business. The lease of the Swan and Hoop and the next door house were due to run out in just over two years, and he seems to have put in Thomas Keats as manager of the former; head ostler and livery stable keeper are later descriptions. Jennings himself moved with his wife Alice to a newly-built house which he rented from a Miss Fuller at Ponder's End, Enfield; he himself continued to receive the rents of the two Moorgate properties.[1] Thomas Keats, whose only daughter Frances Mary was born in 1803, was made free of the Innholders' Company in February, but did not take up his statutory Freedom of the City of London until the end of the year, which may indicate he found some difficulty in paying the fairly large fee; he did not live long to enjoy either, for in the small hours of 15 April 1804, he was killed in a riding accident.

Many speculations have been made over the motives of the next action by Keats's mother; it is perhaps sufficient for the present to observe that she was obviously a creature of impulse (though later remembered as having 'good sense' and 'sensible

[1] MKO.

deportment'), and to notice the material situation she now found herself in. She did not own the public house and stables, the lease of which was anyway due to expire in under a year, on 25 March 1805. The value of her late husband's estate, of which she eventually obtained administration, was under £2000, only just sufficient when invested to pay rent and rates for the Swan and Hoop, let alone support four (possibly five)[1] small children, two of whom, John and George, had already started school. Whatever her motives she married, two and a half months after Thomas Keats's death, William Rawlings, said to be a clerk in a Bank and quite a young man. All that we really know about him is that he paid £1 7s as subscription to a trade directory[2] in which he described himself as livery stable keeper. There is no evidence of his being an innholder, or having anything to do with the business of the inn, though he lived there from his marriage for just under two years until March 1806.

How her father, John Jennings, viewed her action must again be a matter for speculation. When he made his will, seven months after her remarriage, he named as his principal legatees, in order of the capital to be apportioned, his wife Alice, his son Midgley John, Frances, the Keats children, and his own sister Mary Sweetingburgh, who had been widowed in January 1804, her husband leaving her less than £600. John Jennings's will was drawn up in the following form.

> I John Jennings do this first day of February on[3] Thousand Eight hundred & five make this my last Will & Testament in manner & form following (that is to say) that after all my Just Debts shall be duly paid & my Funeral Expenses discharged —
> I give and bequeath to my Wife Alice Jennings Two Hundred Pounds Pr Year being part of the Monies I now have in Bank Security intirely for her own Use & Disposal — together with all my household Furniture & Effects of what nature or kind soever that I may be possessed of at the time of my decease —
> I give & bequeath unto my son Midgley John Jennings Two Thousand Pounds that I have in East India Stock & one thousand nine hundred Pounds being part of the Monies

---

[1] Edward Keats's date of burial is still uncertain, though certainly before February 1805.
[2] *Holden's Triennial Directory 1805-6-7* and for 1808.
[3] For 'one'.

that I have in Bank Security called the new Fives for his use during his natural life & if he should die without Issue I then give & bequeath to his Widow if living at the time of his decease the sum of £500.. — & the remaining part to return to my Family.

I give and bequeath to my daughter Frances Rawlins[1] wife of William Rawlins of St. Stephens Coleman Street Fifty Pounds per year during her natural Life & after her Decease the same to be equally divided among my Grand Children Sons & Daughter of the said Frances Rawlins (that is to say John Keats, George Keats Thomas Keats & Frances Keats Sons & Daughter of the late Thomas Keats —

I give & bequeath to my aforesaid four Grand Children One Thousand Pounds to be equally divided amongst them as they become of Age with the accumulating Interest thereon, & in case either of them should die before they come of Age I then wish & devise that the same may be equally divided among the Survivors —

I give & bequeath to my Sister Mary Sweetingburgh of Old Street in the parish of St. Luke, Thirty Pounds P^r year as long as she may live —

I give & bequeath to Betsy Cousins Daughter of the Above Mary Sweetingburgh (of Lothbury) Five Pounds & to Charles Sweetingburgh Son of the aforesaid Mary Sweetingburgh five Pounds & likewise to Sarah Boswell of Walworth & sister to the above mentioned Charles Sweetingburgh five Pounds —

I give & bequeath to Thomas Baxter of Kensington the Sum of five pounds & likewise to his wife five pounds

I give & bequeath to Henry Nash of Pent[2] Street Bucks the Sum of five Pounds

I do hereby nominate constitute & appoint Charles Danvers of upper Thames Street London & my foresaid Son Midgley John Jennings to be Executors together with my wife Alice Jennings as Executrix of this my last Will & Testament & do hereby revoke all former Wills by me made & declare this to be my last Will & Testament. In Witness whereof I have hereunto set my hand & seal the day of the year first above written.

J^no Jennings

Signed sealed declared &
Delivered in the presence of
    John Robinson
    James Slipper
    Joseph Pearson

---

[1] For 'Rawlings'.   [2] For 'Penn'.

Before discussing the will, it is helpful to see what John Jennings had at his disposal when he made it. The two leasehold Moorgate properties did not, of course, enter into it, since the lease of both was just about to run out. John Jennings's assets were at his death

	£	s	d
East India Stock	1000	0	0
Bank 3% annuities	6493	6	0
3% reduced annuities	2307	10	3
5% annuities 1797 (the 'New Fives')	2013	6	3

There were in addition £24 of short annuities, a mortgage on a property in Knightsbridge due from the executors of Charles Hammond of £1200, and a considerable number of debts owing to him; one of the largest, £150 from John Nattress, was secured by deposit of title deeds of a leasehold property in St George's Fields.

It is easy to see exactly what John Jennings had in mind when he made this will.[1] The Bank 3 per cent annuities and £113 6s 3d of the 'New Fives' would bring in exactly £200 a year for his widow. The remaining £1900 New Fives and the East India Stock he willed specifically to his son. The mortgage when realized would provide £1000 cash for the Keats children; its remaining £200, invested in 3 per cent Bank annuities, which stood on that day at 61[2], would produce £328 of stock; this, added to the £2307 10s 3 per cent reduced annuities, would make a total of £2635 10s 3 per cent stock, and this total plus the £24 short annuities would be just sufficient capital for the annual incomes of £50 and £30 for Frances Rawlings and Mary Sweetingburgh respectively. Minor bequests could be paid out of the debts owed to the estate.

It is essential here to the whole understanding of what follows to make clear two points of simple mathematics. The first relates to stock. The value of stock or capital cannot be treated as the same as its cash value, unless it happens to stand at par; its cash value fluctuates with its market price— as in the example above, when £200 would buy £328 stock,

---

[1] Though this was not how the Court of Chancery finally allocated the stock.

[2] G.M., 1805, Part I, p. 192.

the cash value of that stock was only £200 to its owner. The second point follows. You cannot therefore add cash to capital to produce a cash result, unless you reckon the realizable cash value of that capital at the moment. In brief, nearly all writers on Keats have treated all the stocks involved as if they stood perpetually at par, and have added cash to capital indiscriminately and expressed the result either as cash or capital, thus producing a series of meaningless amounts.[1] The only safe method, which must be followed throughout, is to express capital and cash amounts separately, and always to reckon the current market price of stock when converting it to cash, which can be done easily enough by consulting the daily quotations in the *Gentleman's Magazine*.[2]

John Jennings's will was afterwards criticized by the Master of the Rolls, and later biographers have taken him to task for employing a land-surveyor, Joseph Pearson, to draft it instead of his own attorney, whose name appears to have been Hall.[3] It is quite untrue, however, to assume that this amateur drafting would necessarily lead to Chancery proceedings. There was little in the will that could not have been settled by ordinary solicitors with the good will of all parties. It contained two errors, one particular and one general. The first will probably have been noticed by readers already. For some reason, perhaps failing health, Jennings made an extraordinary mistake about his East India stock. He assumed he had £2000 of it, when he only had in fact £1000. Since he specified the exact type of stock to be left to his son Midgley John, Lieutenant Jennings found himself entitled to only £2900 altogether, instead of the £3900 his father had intended to leave him. The second and general error affected all major legatees. He left ambiguities in the treatment of the capital assigned to both Alice Jennings and Lieutenant Jennings. Did Alice Jennings own the capital that produced her £200 absolutely, only for life or not at all? What happened to Lieutenant Jennings's capital if he died with issue? The will

---

[1] Among many examples, Bate pp. 707, 708 adds £6591 7s 7d *capital* to £772 12s 6d *cash* and produces the meaningless result of 'about £7364' *capital*.

[2] See Appendix V.

[3] He may be the 'Holl' (apparently so written) of one of Keats's letters. Letters, II, p. 228.

only envisaged his dying without issue; this point was of vital concern to the Lieutenant, for on 12 March 1804, he had married at Hartford, near Huntingdon,[1] Margaret Peacock, the daughter of the Rector of Woolley, Hunts, and she was expecting their first child.

John Jennings did not long survive after the will was made. On 8 March he died. The servants were put into mourning, and an expensive funeral took place on 14 March at St Stephen, Coleman Street, where he was buried in the family vault in the North Aisle with the ceremony due to one who had been a respected member of his ward, parish, and City Company. Within his family, however, an uneasy situation prevailed, if we are to judge from later statements. Keats's mother was not an executor; instead, with her mother and brother, John Jennings had nominated Charles Danvers, who had become a neighbour in the Coleman Street parish in 1789.[2] He either did not take, or did not wish to take any part in proving the will, which was thus left solely in the hands of the chief beneficiaries, her brother and mother. Her mother was still at Enfield, her brother out of Town. The situation was a breeding-ground for suspicion; according to her, they were offhand and evasive about the will, even 'sometimes pretending that the said Testator did not make any such Will'.[3] It is impossible to conjecture what part, if any, William Rawlings may have played in this situation. Luckily the boys, John Keats, George, and probably by now their brother Tom, were away at school in the middle of their term. The atmosphere must have been unpleasantly strained.

On Lady Day, 25 March, Lieutenant Jennings came up either from his home in the country or his barracks by coach, charging the fare on the postchaise to his late father's estate. He picked up his mother, and together they went to Doctors' Commons and proved the will,[4] without the help of their other executor, similarly charging the coach-hire to the estate.

[1] Parish register, All Saints, Hartford.
[2] G.L. Ms. 3320.
[3] Appendix I.
[4] On that day, 25 March, they swore that the estate did not amount to more than £12,500; on 26 March Joseph Pearson swore that certain alterations in the wording of the will, made by him, represented John Jennings's intentions. Probate was granted on 27 March.

He then stayed in Town to collect sums due to the estate, and to pay its debts. His sister later claimed that she found him and her mother evasive over the proving of the will and the amount of the estate involved, and it is clear the atmosphere was getting worse. On 1 April, Lieutenant Jennings did something which may have precipitated matters. He collected from his sister and brother-in-law the last quarter's rent on the Swan and Hoop. This, of course, was no more than his duty as executor, since they did not own the property and he was acting for his father who had; it was, in fact, the final quarter of his father's lease, which then expired. The answer to his collecting this quarter's rent seems to have been that William Rawlings presented him with a bill of £41 4s 9d, made out for 'sundry sums' paid by Frances to her own father; Lieutenant Jennings paid this out of the estate on 4 April.

In some circumstances, this might all be taken as the normal settling-up of accounts between relatives in the ordinary course of proving a will and winding-up the affairs of the estate. That it was far from being so in this instance is shown by the events which occurred two days later, on 6 April 1805. On that day, William and Frances Rawlings presented a Bill of Complaint in Chancery[1]

> Humbly complaining shew unto your Lordship your Orator and Oratrix William Rawlings of Moorgate in the City of London Stable Keeper and Frances his wife formerly Frances Jennings Spinster and late Frances Keates widow . . . that the said Midgley John Jennings and the said Alice Jennings or one of them hath possessed the said Testator's personal Estate and Effects and much more than sufficient to answer and satisfy the said Testator's just debts funeral expenses annuities and legacies with a surplus remaining.

They then recite the provisions of the will and the specific legacies, including the bequest to Frances of £50 a year for life, to be divided among the children of her late husband Thomas Keats at her death. The Bill of Complaint then goes on to make a claim whose full weight is not immediately obvious in the wording, though its significance was soon to emerge as one of the chief factors in the subsequent proceedings. William and Frances Rawlings claim

[1] P.R.O., C.13.58.4. See Appendix I for the full text.

that the Testator not having bequeathed nor disposed of the residue of his personal estate died intestate with respect thereto and the same belongs to your Orator and Oratrix in right of your Oratrix Frances Rawlings and to the said Alice Jennings and the said Midgley John Jennings as his next of Kin according to the Statute of Distribution.

In other words, Keats's mother claimed a third share, with her own mother and brother, of all the personal estate that her father had not specifically bequeathed. The sting of this claim, which was to emerge later, lay in what exactly, owing to the ambiguities of the will, was to be regarded as unbequeathed. In support of this claim, the Rawlings asked 'to have an account of the Testator's personal estate and to have the same ascertained and applied as aforesaid'. They then recited the grievances which, they alleged, they had suffered through the conduct of Alice and Lieutenant Jennings over the past few weeks.

For that purpose your Orator and Oratrix have frequently applied . . . and requested them . . . but they . . . refuse to render any such account of the said personal estate sometimes pretending that the said Testator did not make any such Will and at other times they admit that the said Testator made such will and that they have proved the same and possessed themselves of all his personal estate but then they pretend that the same was very small and inconsiderable.

The tone of the Bill then becomes decidedly hostile. 'The said Confederates', as the defendants are now named, are accused not only of this refusal to provide an account of the large estate of John Jennings, but also that

the said Confederates and particularly the said Alice Jennings and Midgley John Jennings or one of them have possessed and converted the same to their own uses without making any satisfaction to your Orator and Oratrix for the said Annuity of fifty pounds so given to your Oratrix for her life as aforesaid and the said Confederates alledge and pretend that your Orator and Oratrix have no right to any account of or interest in the residue of the Testators Estate.

The way that the defendants are alleged to have made this conversion 'to their own uses' is then specified. Alice Jennings

is said to claim not only her £200 annuity but all the capital
producing it and the whole residue of the estate: Midgley
John Jennings is said to claim his capital not only for life but
that his issue on death will be entitled absolutely to it; he also
claims, it is said, equal shares of any undisposed residue with
his co-executor, his mother, both barring any claim by his
sister, who then specifies what her claim actually is.

> Whereas your Orator and Oratrix charge the contrary of all
> such pretences to be true and that the said Confederate Alice
> Jennings under the true construction of the said Will is only
> intitled to two hundred pounds a year for her life

and that John Jennings died intestate with regard to the
capital. Similarly, Frances and William Rawlings claim that
when Midgley John Jennings dies, his capital will pass on as
an intestacy

> and that the confederates the Executors are not intitled to
> such undisposed residue or any part thereof but that the same
> will belong to your Orator and Oratrix in right of your
> Oratrix . . . under the Statute of Distributions and under the
> true construction of the said Will the said Testator never
> intended that the said Confederates the Executors and
> Executrix should take the said residue for their own benefit
> but that the same should go to his family and next of kin and
> that the said confederates the Executors are Trustees thereof
> for the said Testators next of kin

—that is, for Keats's mother, the only next of kin. In brief,
she, with her husband, was claiming that 'under the true
construction of the will', her father had intended her to take a
much greater part of his fortune, and she intended to enforce
this by claiming as next of kin against her mother's and
brother's claim as executors. What she was claiming was a
third share of the capital of approximately £6600 which
would produce her mother's £200 annuity, and, after her
brother's death, a half share of his £2900 capital. Keats's
mother and her husband, in practice, therefore claimed an
immediate £2200 capital and a later £1450 capital, a potential
total, if their Bill was successful, of £3650 capital. She also, of
course, claimed her own annuity of £50 as provided by the
will, and a one-third share of any undisposed cash. It was
certainly a prize worth fighting for.

Whether or not the affair could have been settled in an amicable way, Keats's mother and her husband clearly felt they needed Chancery to construe the will in quite a different way from that in which her mother and brother had apparently interpreted it: since

> All which actings pretences and doings of the said Confederates are contrary to Equity and good conscience and tend to the manifest injury and oppression of your Orator and Oratrix

they felt obliged to apply to Chancery, 'a Court of Equity where matters of this nature are properly cognizable'. Their application particularly asked for a proper account to be taken of the large estate of John Jennings, which they estimate at £12,000, and an explanation of the 'pretences' by which the 'Confederates'—her mother and brother—'refused to comply with such your Orator and Oratrixs requests'. They end by requesting the Court to make an order settling the various main claims of the Bill—that her annuity should be paid out of money properly invested for that purpose by the Court and thus secured to her without the agency of the executors, that the claims of the executors as to capital should be disallowed, that they should be declared trustees for her as the remaining next of kin, and that she should divide the capital equally with them in the ways she had already detailed as 'the true interpretation' of her father's will.

It must surely be observed here that, from this Bill of Complaint, initiated by Keats's mother and her husband as plaintiffs, these are clearly hostile proceedings of a normal kind. They are not merely asking for an obscure will to be construed. They are asking for it to be construed in a particular way which will ultimately put capital of between three and four thousand pounds into their possession. Moreover, they do not base this claim on the obscurity of the will; the intention of the will, they say, is clear, and favours the right of Frances as next of kin. Their need to bring this case to Chancery is not based on the will itself, but, so they allege, on the administration of the will by the executors, her brother and mother. Her mother and brother are named as confederates, with or without the third executor, who have converted parts of the estate without warrant to their own uses, and conspired together to keep her in the dark even about the nature and provisions of the will, not even assuring her of her own named annuity.

How could Colvin have described this as a 'friendly suit'? Part of the answer is, of course, that he never saw the original Bill. He was only given by Thomas 'so much of the will of John Jennings as is set out in the Bill of Complaint'. Yet Thomas had indicated the nature of the proceedings to him if only by using the correct term, Bill of Complaint. Colvin's failure to look at the Bill for himself, followed by every biographer, seems to have led to a basic misunderstanding.

This hostile nature of the Bill certainly does not seem to have been misunderstood by Lieutenant Jennings, if we are to judge by his 'several Answer' to it, made on oath the same day, 6 April 1805.[1] In it, he admitted the will to have been 'to such purport and effect' as set out in the Bill of Complaint, and that he and his mother, without the third executor, had obtained probate of it. He recited the list of John Jennings's holdings, and promised a more exact account of them. He 'believes the complainants may be entitled' to the fifty pounds annuity to his sister for her life. He emphasized his life claim to the East India and £1900 'new Fives' stock, but did not make any further claim for his descendants, merely submitting to the judgment of the Court what should happen to this stock when he himself died with or without issue. He too claimed that the capital producing his mother's annuity was unwilled; but he then claimed, as co-executor, to share it solely with her, and denied his sister any claim on it, or that he was in any way trustee for her. Of all her Bill, in fact, he had only admitted somewhat grudgingly her claim to the £50 annuity. As for her accusations of conspiracy, he pleads against these in emphatic terms which again tend to show clear hostility:

This Defendant denies all unlawful combination and confederacy in and by the said bill charged against him . . . And therefore humbly prays to be hence dismissed with his reasonable costs and charges by him about his suit in this behalf most wrongfully sustained.

---

[1] P.R.O., C.13.58.4. See Appendix II.

Three days later, on 9 April, an Order of the Court of Chancery[1] allowed his mother, Alice Jennings, and the third executor Charles Danvers to put in their 'joint and several answer' without oath, which they did on the same day.[2] In general, this followed the same form as the Lieutenant's answer, with each raising individual points. Charles Danvers stated 'that he hath never proved the said will nor doth he ever intend to prove the same nor hath he possessed any part of the said Testators Estate or effects nor in any manner acted or intermeddled in the said Testators Affairs or concerns'. This did not, of course, let him out from being defendant in the suit. Alice Jennings naturally claimed the capital producing her £200 annuity 'absolutely and for her own use and disposal'; like Lieutenant Jennings, she denied her daughter's claim as next of kin to share in the residue of the estate, and stated that it should be shared solely between herself and her son, Charles Danvers making no claim on it and asking to be discharged from acting in any way concerning the will. As alternative, she made an individual claim of her own that the word 'Effects' in the part of her husband's will relating to her gave her a right to the whole of the unwilled residue, whatever that might eventually be decided to be. Thus both defendants had answered, and made their counter-claims.

When the cause came up for a hearing a month later, on 8 May 1805, before the Master of the Rolls,[3] with Counsel on both sides, Mr Trower for the plaintiffs, Mr Spranger for the defendants, neither side had in any way reduced their claims, which were substantially the same as in the Bill and in the defendants' Answers, except that the former's allegations of conspiracy were perhaps soft-pedalled, Counsel only speaking of 'certain pretences'. Keats's mother's claims on the estate were, however, as large as ever; incidentally, her children's £1000 legacy and the annuity to Mary Sweetingburgh were not mentioned at this hearing. Counsel were heard on both sides, probate of the will was produced, and the Master of the Rolls made his order, an interim one for the production of an account of what was involved. He referred the whole matter to Alexander Popham, 'one of the Masters of this Court'. Popham was to obtain a detailed account of the estate, to advertise for any other next of kin in the *London Gazette*, and to draw up his report on the estate and all the money in the executors' hands; for this purpose the parties to the dispute were ordered to produce to Master Popham 'all books papers or writings in their custody or power relative thereto and are to be examined upon Interrogatories'. In the meantime, all the stock in the estate was to be transferred to the Accountant General. Consideration of the costs of the suit was to be reserved until after Master Popham had made his report.

A feature of the case so far, again perhaps indicating hasty and hostile action, had been the speed of the opening events. John Jennings had hardly been in his grave three weeks before his various next of kin had got in their pleadings on his will, and he had only been dead two months when the first or interlocutory hearing came before the Court. Now, however, the usual delays of Chancery began to take charge, their major cause being that before 1813 the Lord Chancellor had only one judge to assist him, the Master of the Rolls. Over a year was to elapse before the next hearing, time for all parties, and especially Keats's mother, to think what they had done. The estate of John Jennings was now administered by the court of Chancery. It was notoriously more easy to get money into Chancery than to get it out again. Even when the Court ordered that you were entitled to it, it took, to judge from this case, a minimum of two years from the Order to the actual moment when Chancery released the money or stock to you. This was on a principle of serving first those who had won their cause; the losers might, and sometimes did wait for anything up to five years, sometimes even for ever. Keats's mother had an impetuous nature; but she might have remembered that the law is long and life short, especially life in a family of which one member had already died young from tuberculosis. The brutal fact is that by entering into this suit— on whose advice, or whether of her own accord, no one knows— Keats's mother made certain that her own brother did not receive his capital under the will until three months before his own death, and that she herself was not even allocated her capital until a month before she died. Appalling distress was caused to her and her family, and the far-reaching effects on her young children have yet to be examined.

These, headed by John Keats, a boy of nine and a half, were now a major problem during this lull in litigation. Midsummer was approaching when he and the other two boys would return from school. The situation at home was that the lease of the Swan and Hoop had run out, the Rawlings could be turned out by the new owner, Frances's £50 annuity could not be paid to her since all the capital was about to be frozen in Chancery, and the income from her late husband's estate would, as has been seen, only just cover rent and rates. What William Rawlings could provide we do not know; certainly he had no capital. What happened at Midsummer must be conjecture, except that it was some sort of cataclysm for the children. At Midsummer, Alice Jennings, their grandmother, left her rented house at Ponders End, and rented another in Church Street, Edmonton. Her landlord was a victualler and innholder,[1] probably an old business friend, and her neighbour there was the surgeon and apothecary Thomas Hammond, who had attended her husband in his last illness,[2] and who afterwards took John Keats as apprentice, the choice becoming obvious now it is known that he already was the family doctor. It was to Edmonton, according to Keats's sister remembering the event in her old age,[3] that Alice Jennings took her four grandchildren to live with her, while their mother and stepfather continued for the time to live at the Swan and Hoop.

Under what emotional or physical circumstances the transfer of the Keats children took place at this time, we simply do not know. It is to be remarked that the parties to it, their mother and her own mother, were engaged in a suit where one had first accused the other of fraudulent conspiracy and then claimed a large share of the other's inheritance. It can be seen that these feelings and attitudes were still present this

---

[1] KSMB, XII, p. 26, 'John Keats: Further Notes', Phyllis Mann.
[2] P.R.O., C.38.957.
[3] Keats House Collection, No. 61. 'Edmonton' instead of 'Enfield' fixes the date, and though she says elsewhere 'My Brothers and myself never lived with them, but always with my grandmother' (F.K.L.), the fact that she does not mention her grandfather tends to confirm that the move was not made till after his death.

summer by something which also seems to confirm that the suit itself was very far from 'friendly'. On 8 September, with the law still in its summer delay, Lieutenant Jennings advanced out of the cash in the estate (dividends, repaid debts etc.) £100 to his mother for her half-year's annuity from her husband's death to that date. He made absolutely no attempt to pay his sister any of her £50 annuity and in fact never did so until compelled three years later by an Order in Chancery.[1] When one adds the thought that the Lieutenant was a schoolboy hero to the boys, especially to John Keats, the effect of the whole situation, which could not have been kept from an intelligent boy of nearly ten, may have been enormous. We must remember that the era was one when emotion over family affairs played far greater part in people's lives than it might now. Everyone behaved with much less reticence, everything was discussed before the children, expression was free and violent and demonstrative; the personal behaviour of Nelson, for instance, was not that of an abnormal genius, but that of a typical person of his time.[2] Though there were other and obvious factors, we need look no further than the situation created by the Chancery suit to account for Keats's almost total reticence about his family and the 'earlier Misfortunes' he once mysteriously spoke about. To know what this family conflict did for him, we should need to know more about how a poet is made; but at least we need no longer guess at the material basis of the conflict.

To return to Master Popham, in whose hands the suit now lay: he had, of course, to see whether advertisements in the London Gazette produced any other claimant on the estate or next-of-kin, but even then there seems to have been a long gap in proceedings until 23 November 1805, when he endorsed the Plaintiffs' Interrogatories as allowed. Two days later he also allowed that if necessary Lieutenant Jennings should be examined on these Interrogatories by Commission, 'the said Defendant living remote in the country'.[3] As he was a serving officer in time of war—it was only a month after Trafalgar—this involved his examination on the Interrogatories taking

---

[1] P.R.O., C.33.562. f. 1146.
[2] White, R. J., *Life in Regency England*, p. 9.
[3] P.R.O., C.38.942.

place at Rochester, near to where he was stationed at Chatham. His deposition had to be taken before Commissioners and Counsel representative of the parties in the suit, an expedition to Kent which must have increased the costs of the case. Lieutenant Jennings's answer was deemed sufficient, since his mother filed an affidavit that she had not 'intermeddled' with the estate.

His sworn Reply,[1] which has never been reproduced or examined before,[2] provides incidentally a great deal of the new biographical detail which has been incorporated earlier in this book in the account of the Jennings and Keats families. It also provided Popham with detailed executors' accounts and statements of John Jennings's funds, which he was able to incorporate in his Report for the Court, though this once more took some time. The accounts, which must have been difficult enough for the Lieutenant, with his professional duties, to handle were necessarily of an interim nature. No bill had yet been obtained, for example, for the funeral expenses. A large number of debts, some perhaps not recoverable, were still owing to the estate, a witness to the wide nature of the business carried on by John Jennings up to his death. While Popham was reducing these to some sort of order for his report, the matter of handing over the stock into Chancery went on. On 10 February 1806, Lieutenant Jennings transferred into the name of the Accountant General all his father's stock and annuities except the East India Stock, which was transferred three days later, and on 28 February his accounts as presented in his examination were confirmed by the Accountant General. It was now time for Popham to present his Report, which he did on 6 March, nearly a year after John Jennings had died. He set out the stock, the money in the Lieutenant's hands, the payments out, and the debts outstanding in four schedules, often giving more exact particulars than the Lieutenant had done. The largest item in the fourth schedule, of debts outstanding, was the £1200 mortgage, which had still not come in. He concluded that the cash in the Lieutenant's hands was £1005 10s 1d and the debts so far

---

[1] P.R.O., C.13.502. Rawlings v. Jennings. See Appendix IV.
[2] Ralph Thomas seems to have based his notes on the subsequent Report.

paid £424 15s 5d, leaving a personal estate of £580 14s 8d,[1] which passed under an intestacy.[1]

The stage was therefore now set for a decision on the much larger question whether there was an intestacy relating to the greater part of the capital, and whether Keats's mother had any right to it. Popham's Report having been ratified and confirmed on 8 March,[2] the cause came up for its hearing[3] on 22 May 1806. After the arguments by Counsel on both sides, the Master of the Rolls ordered that the cause should stand for judgment. During the two month delay which then ensued, while all parties waited for judgment, it is interesting to note an action of Lieutenant Jennings. On 5 July, he made yet another advance to his mother out of the money in his hands so that she should not feel the want of her annuity pending the Court's decision. Once more, there was no attempt to pay his sister any of hers, and he paid his mother not only the £166 13s 4d which was due to her for the ten months since the last payment, but an extra £23 6s 8d.[4] This suggests that Alice Jennings, now with four small grandchildren on her hands, and school fees to pay for three of them, was finding things difficult, and that he was prepared to help out her, though not his sister.

On 29 July 1806, judgment was given by the Master of the Rolls. The decision was entirely in favour of Alice Jennings with regard to the absolute ownership of her stock. The Master of the Rolls underlined this by pointing out that her husband's words in the will allotting her 'part of the Monies I now have in Bank Security intirely for her own Use & Disposal' gave her specific and absolute possession of these named securities, in contrast with the definite limitation of the words 'during her natural life' only, applied to the unnamed stock producing her daughter's annuity. Although Alice Jennings was disallowed her extra claim that the 'Effects' meant the unwilled residue too, that unwilled residue was to be divided between her and the Lieutenant; Frances had failed in that claim too as next-of-kin, and was left with nothing but her

---

[1] P.R.O., C.38.957.
[2] P.R.O., C.33.543.
[3] Vesey, XIII, pp. 39–47.
[4] P.R.O., C.38.1005.

right to a £50 annuity. She had, perhaps, a slight hope of eventual claim on her brother's capital, since the Master decided to 'declare the son entitled during his life; with liberty upon his death for any party, who is interested, to apply', but with the way judgment had just gone against her, her prospect of a share of his capital on his death would be negligible. From her point of view, the action initiated by her Bill of Complaint had failed.[1]

It is clear too that about this time, or a little earlier, her second marriage had failed also; whether the two events were in any way connected one does not know. The rate books for the Swan and Hoop suggest that she left Rawlings rather than that he left her, and that this took place shortly before an innholder named Joshua Vevers took over the lease and occupation on 25 March 1806.[2] What happened to her then is unknown. She would hardly return to her mother, with the issue of the hostile suit she had brought against her still pending; this gives more colour than has sometimes been allowed to the report[3] that she lived with another man, for she would at this stage be without money or home. As for Rawlings, there is probably truth in the same report that he died in a short time, possibly, it seems, after about three years. The often-repeated statement that he was still alive in 1825, because his name still appears in the Chancery suit then, is based on a misunderstanding of Chancery procedure. In every order of Chancery, the names of the parties making the original pleadings, the original Plaintiffs and Defendants, are always written at the head of all subsequent proceedings. The final order in December 1825 is headed, like all others, with the names of William and Frances Rawlings as Plaintiffs, Midgley John Jennings and Alice Jennings as Defendants; all the other three were by then long dead, and there is no reason to doubt that Rawlings was also.

Certainly the Order in Chancery[4] which was issued on the same day as the judgment gave Keats's mother little hope of assistance for some time. It was the business of the Court to

[1] Vesey, XIII, pp. 45–47.
[2] G.L. Ms. 4489/1.
[3] KC, I, p. 305.
[4] P.R.O., C.33.546. f. 1153.

settle first the claims of the Defendants, which had been allowed, and to look after the Plaintiffs later. The East India Stock and the £1900 'New Fives' were to be transferred to Lieutenant Jennings, 'subject to further order of this Court'. Alice Jennings got her order for the transfer of capital to her, outright, though not in the apportionments her husband had perhaps imagined. She was to receive the remainder (£113 6s 3d) of the 'New Fives', the whole £2307 10s of the Bank 3 per cent reduced, and as much of the Bank 3 per cent ordinary as would totally bring in her £200 annuity; in practice this proved to be £4170 11s 4d, leaving £2322 14s 8d in the hands of the Court to meet the further contingencies of the will. She was also allotted, like Lieutenant Jennings, half the residue of the estate, which at that moment stood altogether at £580 14s 8d cash; this would be paid when the estate's accounts should finally be settled, including the paying of the considerable costs of the suit, which would be subtracted from it.

Yet even this comprehensive decision and allocation in favour of the Defendants was, owing to the delays of the law, a mixed blessing which must have brought bitterness and distress. For, in the event, the transfer of his stock to the Lieutenant was not made by the Accountant General until another two whole years had passed, on 2 August 1808. His mother received hers nine days later.[1] If he, as the successful defendant, was put to such straits—and, as will be seen, the whole situation may have been literally fatal to him—the result was even worse for his sister, the plaintiff. All the Court ordered on 29 July 1806 was that it should be seen how much of the remaining 3 per cent stock would be necessary to produce her annuity of £50; there was no guarantee when this would be done, or how long would elapse before she would actually draw the annuity. A similar order was made over the £30 annuity for someone whom all the litigants seemed to have forgotten, John Jennings's sister, Mary Sweetingburgh. There was also a provision in the order to compute interest on the £1000 legacy for the Keats children, but again no hint of when this might be set aside for them; indeed, it could not have been at that moment, since the Lieutenant had not yet been able to obtain payment of the mortgage owing to his

[1] P.R.O., C.38.1005.

father which was to provide it. As for the legal representatives, a sum of £231 17s. cash was put aside to cover costs, to be assessed later, for William Walton, of Walton and Gliddon, Keats's mother's solicitor, and for John Shaddick, the defendants' clerk in Court.[1] The total costs were eventually much more than this sum.

The burden of anxiety and responsibility during this waiting period now naturally fell on the Lieutenant, as his father's sole acting executor. The debts to the estate were slow in coming in, especially the two largest, the mortgage and the debt of John Nattress, though he collected interest on both. He had to diminish the ready cash in his hands by two more payments, during the year 1807, to his mother, to make up for the annuity for whose capital she was still waiting. At the end of that year, worry and legal action had done what the naval action with the Dutch off Camperdown had failed to do; at New Year, 1808, the Lieutenant went sick from Chatham barracks.[2] Four months later, he was applying for another month's sick leave, and the Huntingdon surgeon's report sounded an ominous note; the Lieutenant was coughing blood. His responsibility to all branches of his family was heavy; his fourth child, Walter John, had just been baptized.[3] Somehow he struggled on, and in June he had the satisfaction of receiving the last two large debts to his father's estate. In July, he was promoted Captain—promotion was slow in the Marines—and early in August he at last received his capital, and took up his new appointment at Woolwich.

At this moment, initiated by his sister again, the Chancery cause sprang once more to life, fully bearing out the dictum of a legal authority that whereas in other courts 'the whole of the litigation is normally finished as soon as judgment is pronounced, in the usual Chancery action it has barely begun'.[4] On a motion made by her Counsel, Mr Trower, before the Lord High Chancellor on 11 August 1808, Keats's mother

---

[1] P.R.O., C.33.546. f. 1153.

[2] KSR.

[3] Hartford Parish Register, Baptisms, 6 April, 1808. His name was hitherto thought to be William, possibly owing to some confusion with a posthumously-born William, who, like him, died young. KSMB, XIV, p. 29. 'A cousin of Keats', William A. W. Jarvis.

[4] *Odgers' Principles of Practice and Pleading*, 17th ed. 1960, p. 343.

claimed that Captain Jennings should pay to her out of the money now in his hands her £50 annuity for two years up to 8 March 1807.[1] He had, indeed, made no attempt to do so, in contrast with his solicitude for their mother; since the estate was now fully solvent, his own Counsel, Mr Spranger, could hardly do more than consent, and the Order was accordingly made. Nothing in this fresh move suggests any reconciliation or mutual arrangement between brother and sister over this payment of £100, which she did not receive from him until 5 September.[2] It was the last bit of business he was to be concerned with, apart from a codicil to his own will on 20 November, for on 21 November he died at the early age of thirty-one.

Whatever personal conclusions might be drawn from this tragedy, the legal position was that his responsibilities were now taken over by his executors, the widow Margaret Jennings, her sister Mary Maxwell and Charles John Wye, who seems initially to have been sole acting executor, though death removed even him soon. Wye had on his hands the personal cash accounts of the estate of John Jennings, to be presented finally to Master Popham, though he too disappeared from the cause at about this time, either by death or retirement, his place being taken by another Master of the Court. Wye had also, as executor, to restore into the Court the East India Stock and the 'New Fives', only acquired from the Accountant General of the Court a few months before, and now inevitably to be the subject of further litigation. Moreover, he had to execute Midgley John Jennings's own will, which was complicated by the fact that it had to envisage the various ways Chancery might decide to dispose of the capital left him by his father's will, with its uncertain provisions in the case of own death. There is no wonder that practically the last act of Midgley John Jennings's life had been, by a codicil to this will, to remove one original executor and to substitute Wye, a Lincoln's Inn solicitor.[3] It will be remembered too that the Judgment of 29 July 1806 had only assigned him his capital for life 'with liberty upon his death for any

[1] P.R.O., C.33.562. f. 1146.
[2] P.R.O., C.38.1005.
[3] Principal Probate Registry, Loveday, 114.

party, who is interested, to apply'. These parties might include Keats's mother and her husband if they chose to revive their original Bill of Complaint against Wye as executor, it having 'abated', in legal terms, at her brother's death. They did so on 29 April 1809,[1] though not in very positive terms, merely claiming to have against Wye 'the same Relief as they would have been entitled to if the said Midgley John Jennings had been living'. In fact, they do not seem to have put in any application for a share of Midgley John Jennings's capital. Moreover, when Wye himself put in a petition for some of Midgley John Jennings's cash interest held by Chancery, it was recorded on 16 May 1809,[2] 'no one appeared on behalf of the parties altho' duly served with a copy of the said petition'. There is also support for the idea that at this time, Keats's mother became at last reconciled to her own family, and that this is the time when she returned to her grandmother's house, and to her four children. On 8 July, she petitioned that Wye should pay her, out of the cash residue which had been in her brother's hands, two more years' annuity, up to 8 March 1809. She was said to be 'in great distress' and made this special motion since, owing to the press of business in Chancery, 'there is no probability of obtaining an Order in time to procure payment under it previous to the Michaelmas term'. It was said that 'it is the wish of all parties that this may be paid out' and these 'parties', of course, included her own mother. The difference in tone of the hearing thus recorded in the Order which gave her this money,[3] so different from any previous hearing including her own previous application for the first two years' annuity from her brother,[4] might seem to indicate a change of attitude all round and a family reconciliation, as indeed would be natural after the death of her brother. Alice Jennings was ageing—she was now seventy-two —and Frances, ominously, was already ill; of the Keats children her eldest son John was thirteen and a half, and had just won his first prize at school. The tremendous burst of intellectual activity in him, which was noted by everyone at

[1] P.R.O., C.33.568. f. 507.
[2] P.R.O., C.33.568. f. 546.
[3] P.R.O., C.33.569. f. 715.
[4] P.R.O., C.33.562. f. 1146.

his school as beginning at this time, might well be put down to the return of his mother, and not, as it has been, to her death when it occurred tragically soon afterwards. It may be yet another instance of the fatal process Keats mentioned much later in a letter: 'I have never known any unalloy'd Happiness for many days together: the death or sickness of someone has always spoilt my hours'.[1]

The order of 8 July 1809 also helped to rescue from distress someone unrepresented in the case, and hitherto almost forgotten, John Jennings's sister, Mary Sweetingburgh. She had not received a penny of her annuity since her brother's death, and four years' arrears was now belatedly paid to her. It was becoming time to regularize the many outstanding matters in the case, and the new Master who had taken over from Popham had just presented his report.[2] Its immediate result, indeed, was only an apportionment of costs to the legal representatives for the first section of the case; William Walton, Keats's mother's solicitor, received £114 18s 8d out of the estate, and John Shaddick, the defendants' clerk in Court, £98 11s 9d. This was only, so to speak, a first instalment for the initial processes of the action. When subsequent costs were added and finally paid out in March 1812,[3] Walton's total costs were £242 11s 5d and Shaddick's £185 9s 3d. The whole case therefore cost the litigants about £428, or something like a round £3000 in modern terms.

There was still enough, however, in the estate to provide for the remaining requirements of the will, and this report at last set out how this should be done. £1666 13s 4d of 3 per cent stock would produce the annuity for Keats's mother, £1000 stock the annuity for Mary Sweetingburgh. The sum of £1000 cash could now at last be allocated to the Keats children, since the large mortgage owing to the estate had come in; in fact, the cash assets of the estate now stood at the healthy figure of £1738 14s 8d, out of which Wye paid almost at once the back annuities to Keats's mother and to Mary Sweetingburgh, before paying the cash residue into Court. The successive ways in which this cash residue of the estate

---

[1] Letters, II, p. 123.
[2] P.R.O., C.38.1005.
[3] Ralph Thomas Ms.

was diminished in the next year or so need not be detailed, but one point must be emphasized. When all payments had been made out of it, this cash was what the Court reckoned to be the clear cash residue of the estate, as defined by the Judgment of 1806. Various other sums—the back payments of annuities and interest, for instance—have been confused with this, but it remains the cash residue as that term is used by the Court. When all such payments had been made, this cash in Court stood at £497 5s plus a further £37 16s 2d—a total of £535 1s 2d. It was eventually divided equally between Alice Jennings and the executors of her son in two payments, to each party, of £248 12s 6d and £18 18s 1d each,[1] being then defined as 'clear residue', a total of £267 10s 7d each. It is important in the subsequent financial history of the Keats children to regard this £267 10s 7d, and this only, as their grandmother's ultimate share of the cash residue of their grandfather's estate.

Meanwhile, a fresh element was precipitated into the case by another set of grandchildren. Midgley John Jennings's capital, the East India and 5 per cent stock, had of course on his death remained in Chancery, 'with liberty upon his death for any party who is interested, to apply'. On 8 December 1809, application was made in a petition by his widow, Margaret Jennings.[2] Much has been speculated about a Chancery action which this Margaret Jennings, Keats's aunt by marriage, is said to have threatened in 1819, and which he mentions in his letters; here, for the first time, is evidence that she certainly took Chancery action nearly ten years earlier. She petitioned, however, not on behalf of herself, but for her children, Keats's cousins, Margaret Alice, Midgley John (junior) and Mary Ann;[3] the others, Walter John and William, had evidently died in infancy. She claimed on their behalf that they were 'entitled absolutely' to the whole of their late father's valuable East India and 5 per cent stock. It must be remembered that she was a country clergyman's daughter trying to bring up three small children on a Marine Captain's pension.

---

[1] P.R.O., C.33.585. f. 1041, and Ralph Thomas Ms.
[2] P.R.O., C.33.576. f. 417.
[3] So baptized: registers, All Saints, Hartford, 9 August 1807. In various Chancery orders she appears as Meriam and Maurice.

This was only one new element in many unsettled aspects of the cause when it came up for further judgment before the Lord Chancellor on 13 February 1810, some five years after John Jennings had made his disputed will. The Order[1] consequent on this judgment is the most important of the whole cause, so far as it affected Keats's future, except perhaps the Order dismissing the claims of his mother's original Bill. It will be remembered that in that Order of 1806, £2322 14s 8d had been left of John Jennings's 3 per cent Consolidated Bank Annuities.[2] £1666 13s 4d of this was now set aside for Keats's mother to produce £50 a year, her one back annuity from 8 March 1809 also being paid to her. The remaining £656 1s 4d had added to it £343 18s 8d of 3 per cent stock, bought with £221 16s 9d from the cash residue of the estate, the 3 per cent stock then standing on the market at 64½. The £1000 stock thus produced gave Mary Sweetingburgh her annuity of £30.

It was now time to turn to the two sets of grandchildren. First, the petition brought in the name of the Jennings grandchildren was dismissed. The late Captain's stock was to be divided 'in equal moieties' between his widow as executor and his mother Alice Jennings, £1450 of 5 per cent stock and £500 East India stock to each. This, for the Jennings children, was only half a loaf. The gap of silence and non-recognition between Keats and his cousins may be traced to this, if not to earlier proceedings, for the Keats grandchildren were fully and explicitly catered for. 'It is decreed that the sum of £1000 be laid out in the purchase of 3 per cent Consolidated Bank Annuities in the name and with the privity of the Accountant General' in trust for them; moreover, 'on their respectively attaining their Ages of 21 years they are to be at liberty to apply to this Court for transfers of their respective shares . . . as they shall be advised.'

It is as well to be quite clear what this purchase meant to the children in terms of stock. It meant that their total amount of 3 per cent stock, bought at the market price of 64½,[3] was £1550 7s 10d, a quarter of which each of the children could

---

[1] P.R.O., C.33.576. f. 417.
[2] See *ante*, p. 25
[3] Purchased by the Accountant General on 30 April 1811 at the same time as Mary Sweetingburgh's stock.

apply for on coming of age, with his or her share of the interest to that date. This sum of £1550 7s 10d stock is to be borne in mind, since it confused Colvin and even Ralph Thomas, who told Colvin it represented £1000 plus interest.[1] It is, quite simply, what stock the Court could buy at the current market price with the Keats children's cash legacy. Since they also each had a quarter share in their mother's £1666 13s 4d stock after her death, each Keats child could apply to Chancery at the age of twenty-one for one quarter of a total of £3217 1s 2d stock: that is, £804 5s 3½d stock each, plus cash interest. In brief, at any time after twenty-one by applying 'as they shall be advised', any one of them could become the absolute owner of just over £800 3 per cent stock.

In fact, such was the further tragic course of events, that the Keats children became almost at once potential claimants, when they should reach twenty-one, for this whole property. Their mother did not survive the granting of the capital for her annuity for more than a month. In this ill-starred case, the same fate overtook her as had overtaken her brother, and on 20 March she was buried in the family vault after dying of the family disease, a 'decline'. The effect of this on John Keats, now at the age of fourteen, has been fully explored in conjecture. In barely six years, early deaths had deprived him of a father, stepfather (probably), a mother and an uncle, the last two having been for much of that time locked in a dispute that may well have hastened their end.

The sole stable member of the family, the sole gainer by the Chancery suit that had been started against her, was now Keats's grandmother, Alice Jennings. She had lost husband, son, daughter; but she had, potentially or in existing fact, wrested from Chancery a total of £8541 7s 7d capital stock[2] and £267 10s 7d cash residue as her absolute property. She was determined that it should not get into Chancery again, and that it should be used largely for the benefit of her dead daughter's four children. She therefore on 30 July 1810 executed a deed or indenture dealing with the whole of this capital and residue, which she made over to two business men

---

[1] He, however, stated it correctly in the accounts. Appendix VII.
[2] Including her £500 share of Mary Sweetingburgh's £1000 stock. See *post*, p. 33.

John Nowland Sandell, a merchant, and Richard Abbey, a wholesale tea dealer. Though the deed is lost, its nature is fully set out in an Order of Chancery nearly five years later,[1] when her trustees obtained from Chancery the last of the capital mentioned in it, the half of the £1000 stock producing her sister-in-law's, Mary Sweetingburgh's annuity. The estate thus handed over to the two trustees consisted of everything Alice Jennings had received or was to receive from her husband's will or by any order of Chancery. It consisted, as has been said, of the whole £8541 7s 7d capital stock and the cash residue of £267 10s 7d, and it was assigned to the trustees in the most absolute terms:

> from thenceforth as and for their own Monies and Effects in as full large and ample a manner to all intents and purposes whatsoever as she the said Alice Jennings her executors or administrators might or could have done if the said recited Indenture had not been made upon the several Trusts in the said Indenture mentioned for the benefit of John Keats George Keats Thomas Keats and Frances Mary Keats Grandchildren of the said Alice Jennings after the Determination of the Life Interest the said Trust premised thereby limited to the said Alice Jennings.

In other words, reserving only her life interest, her considerable estate, stock and cash, would not appear in her will, nor come up for declaration or probate, but would become automatically and absolutely the property of the two trustees to administer for the grandchildren according to the provisions of various trusts in the Indenture. The two same trustees became, by her will of the next day, also the executors of that, to dispose of the very small personal residue which would now be left, in the event less than £450.[2] Misunderstanding of this deed or indenture has led to the trustees and executors being accused of dishonesty, and the small figure of £450 sworn for the will being doubted. In fact, the formation of such a trust was perfectly legal,[3] and its intention obvious: to prevent a disputed will, with claims on it by her son's

---

[1] P.R.O., C.33.616. f. 809.

[2] Principal Probate Registry, Effingham, 193.

[3] Her son, perhaps for the same motives, formed a similar trust. His executor also swore to a very small personal estate. P.P.R., Loveday, 114.

widow or anyone else. Alice Jennings had had enough of such experiences.

The Keats children therefore now had from this date, 30 July 1810, two quite distinct and separate sets of property being held in trust for them. On the one hand, each Keats child had, as we have seen, just over £800 stock held in trust by the Accountant General of the Court of Chancery, to be applied for with its cash interest at the age of twenty-one. On the other hand, each child now had its share of property from their grandmother, which she had received from Chancery and had placed by indenture in the hands of their trustees, Sandell and Abbey. Much confusion has been caused by previous writers trying to trace the later history of these two quite different funds as if they were one; it has therefore seemed best here to treat them, as their nature demands, quite apart. Consideration of the trust for the children set up by Alice Jennings, and administered by Sandell and Abbey, is postponed till later in this study,[1] so that we can now finish tracing the legacies of John Jennings still being administered by Chancery.

The next few years were mainly concerned with reports, certificates and orders putting into practice the main Order of 13 February 1810. The residue of the estate was substantially reduced by being drawn on for the £1000 cash to buy the Keats children their stock. When it was invested for them on 30 April 1811, it had accumulated £185 3s 8d interest,[2] ear-marked to their mother by the Order of 13 February 1810 for their maintenance and education; but as their mother was by then dead, it was not applied. The next year, 1812, saw the payment of their final costs to William Walton, solicitors for the plaintiffs, and John Shaddick, clerk in Court for the defendants. It now appeared that no further complication could ensue, and that John Keats, now entered on a medical training as apprentice to the surgeon who had attended his grandfather, Thomas Hammond, was fully assured of his capital of £800 or so from Chancery when he was twenty-one, just about when he might be presumed to be setting up in practice himself. There was, however, one disquieting incident,

[1] See p. 42.
[2] P.R.O., C.38.1037.

though it may not have seemed so at the time. On 4 December 1813, Mary Sweetingburgh, Keats's great-aunt, died at the age of eighty. She had, of course, for the last few years of her life received her annuity of £30 from the £1000 stock held in Chancery for her. At her death, both Alice Jennings and Midgley John Jennings's widow could apply for it. Neither immediately did. With Captain Jennings's widow, there is a possible reason; her co-executor, who had so far acted solely in this case, the Lincoln's Inn solicitor Charles John Wye, had himself died. She and her own sister, Mary Maxwell, were now surviving executors, and without Wye there may not have been anyone immediately to advise them.[1]

No similar reason could be urged to explain why Keats's grandmother did not apply. She had been fully in touch with a solicitor who knew every detail of the Chancery case, and who had, in fact, done extremely well out of it; for Alice Jennings had employed to draw up her own will and trust deed William Walton, who had been her daughter's solicitor in the cause. Although he had appeared for her daughter, the plaintiff, against her, he may well have seemed after her daughter's death a natural and good choice. He knew every move of the case since its first Bill of Complaint in April 1805, he had endorsed many of its documents; since her concern was for her daughter's children, she chose someone who must have known the precise details of all the stock and funds involved, and exactly what all the Keats children were due to receive from Chancery.

Walton, however, does not seem to have advised her that she could apply to Chancery for her share in Mary Sweetingburgh's capital, on the latter's death. A year passed before Alice Jennings herself died, and still she had not applied. Application was made after her death by her two executors and trustees, John Nowland Sandell and Richard Abbey. They and her son's two surviving executors, Margaret Jennings and Mary Maxwell, petitioned the Court of Chancery on 19 April 1815, for a decision of the Court solely on this matter

---

[1] On the other hand, Wye had died before 26 July 1811, and this had not prevented Margaret Jennings and Mary Maxwell from getting the cash residue. Their application had, however, been put in before his death.

of Mary Sweetingburgh's capital. On 10 May 1815, it was allotted to the two sets of executors in two equal parts of £500 stock each, together with equal shares of the interest that had accrued since Mary Sweetingburgh's death during the time when no one had applied.[1] Walton acted in this hearing, and in fact his clerk, Philip Hurd, swore an affidavit.[2] The hearing took place when John Keats was just finishing his apprenticeship to Hammond, and preparing to go to Guy's Hospital, which he entered on 1 October 1815 when he was nearly twenty. The next year saw his qualification for medicine by becoming a Licentiate of the Society of Apothecaries, his first published poem, and his enthusiastic recognition by the literary world of Leigh Hunt and others. On 31 October 1816 he was twenty-one. Although still attending surgical lectures and practising surgery, he felt himself temperamentally unsuited for the job, and his poetic success had, in the words of a fellow-student, 'sealed his fate'. Now was the time for him to apply for his £800-odd capital from Chancery, which by this time had acquired £168 17s 6d cash interest. It was at any rate a foundation for the independent life of a poet.

He did not apply. In fact, it is clear that he never knew the money was there in Chancery, only waiting for his application. A scapegoat has been sought for this extraordinary and tragic error, and for some reason almost universal blame has been laid on the trustee of Keats's quite separate other trust, the one formed by his grandmother and now in the hands of Richard Abbey, the other trustee John Nowland Sandell having been buried on 18 May 1816.[3] Even those who have condemned Abbey for supposedly concealing the existence of the Chancery trust fund from Keats have expressed puzzlement at his motives and concluded that 'there is no accounting for his action', since he could not possibly gain by it himself. The perfectly simple fact is that there is absolutely no evidence whatsoever that Abbey knew of the funds in Chancery, or that Keats could apply for them at twenty-one. Abbey had never been concerned in any capacity with the stock held in

[1] P.R.O., C.33.616. f. 809.
[2] P.R.O., C.31.360/1.
[3] KSMB, XIII, p. 27. 'Mrs Jennings' Will', Norman Kilgour.

trust for the Keats children in Chancery by the Accountant General. His one connection with the Chancery cause, on 10 May 1815, had been as executor to Alice Jennings, and had been strictly confined to the capital of Mary Sweetingburgh. In that hearing, no mention whatsoever had been made in Court or elsewhere of the capital held by the Accountant General for the Keats children.[1] The plain answer to the question why Abbey did not tell Keats about it is that he did not himself know.

There was, however, someone who did. Without attributing to him the sinister and perverse conduct which has been invented for Abbey, one would like to know why William Walton the solicitor did not inform Keats. He had, as had been seen, entered into every aspect of the case, and had drawn very good fees in it. In this may lie the reason for his extraordinary negligence, though we should not perhaps press it as proof. A study of Walton's own will,[2] however, provides some interesting thought. He first drew it up for himself in 1806, when the case of Rawlings v. Jennings, in which he was plaintiffs' solicitor, was getting under way. Five years later, on 26 October 1811, when he had just drawn most of his considerable fees for the case, Walton added a codicil to his will. He did this very explicitly 'in consequence of the change of circumstances' since 1806. In that time, his circumstances had improved so much that he had been able to build a new house in Epping Forest and to buy very considerable additional land and property. Walton attributed this success to Divine providence, which is given its due in his codicil: 'for which I offer up in humble submission my most grateful thanks to the all gracious and bountiful disposer of all things'. One may think that if his firm had many clients like Keats's mother, such pious thanks were hardly necessary. The exact coincidence between the Chancery case and his own prosperity is certainly startling; added to this, he drew up his own will with such confusion, and so many further codicils, that it took ten years after his death for his son and namesake, his successor in the firm of Walton and Gliddon, to sort it out. Without making him a villain, one may think

[1] P.R.O., C.33.616. f. 809.
[2] Principal Probate Registry, Ellenboro 449.

that, in his new fortune, any advice to or application for the Keats children might seem very small beer in the way of fees, and that on the evidence of his own will, he appears a bungler. Whatever the true explanation, it was a disaster, and not only for John Keats. On 28 February 1818, his brother George came of age. He too had his urgent necessities. He was unhappy in business, and he had decided to marry and emigrate to America. His life might have taken an entirely different course, or his circumstances might have been eased, if someone had advised him to apply to Chancery for his £800 capital which had now accumulated for him a cash interest of about £205. Even if he had still emigrated, this might have enabled him to tide over the financial difficulties he almost at once got into, and which, in their turn, vitally affected John Keats, as will be seen later.[1] Tom Keats, the third brother, was saved this ironic situation by dying on 1 December 1818, when he was only just nineteen. Now, if ever, some advice should have been offered to Keats. If he had applied, there is no doubt that Chancery would have awarded him not only his own portion, but a third share of his dead brother's stock and cash interest. This meant that in December 1818, he could have obtained £1072 capital and £266 8s cash.

Still ignorant of this fund at his disposal, Keats now found himself, all through the year 1819, in severe financial stress. During the early months he existed by drawing on money that George had left behind in England.[2] By the early summer this was gone, mostly on living expenses and rent for the house at Hampstead he now shared with Charles Brown. Prompted by the latter, Keats now began a somewhat unsystematic campaign of trying to call in the loans, estimated by Brown at £200, he had made to other people. In this he was only partly successful, and he found himself frequently forced to borrow from Brown, oblivious of the £1072 capital and its interest, by now about £300, only waiting for his application in Chancery.

Worse was to follow. In the winter of 1819–20, George's financial difficulties in America became so acute that he returned to England to raise all available cash. Unfortunately

---

[1] See p. 51.
[2] See *post*, p. 50.

he, like Keats, was totally unaware of his own £1072 capital and £300 cash in Chancery. All he knew of was the trust fund set up by their grandmother, and administered by Abbey. From this he drew not only what remained to him, but most of what might still have come to Keats. This was probably only a fair squaring of this particular account between the two brothers,[1] but there is evidence Keats felt it deeply. Only a day or two after George left England, Keats had the haemorrhage which heralded his end, very likely accelerated by his financial worries, over himself and George, both of which could have been obviated by simple application to Chancery.

When one thinks of the stresses of mind and body which Keats is known to have suffered during these years of his short life, no other comment is needed on these facts and figures. Much money from many causes is known to have lain unclaimed in Chancery at this period, but the results can seldom have been such a tragedy for poetry. The whole story is made even more ironic by the fact that the inheritance did not lie there for ever. When George Keats was twenty-five, four years late even by his own reckoning, he became aware of the fact of the Chancery funds and applied for his share of them, which was allowed him by an Order in Chancery of 21 March 1823.[2] Even here, to the surviving Keats brother, there was an ironic detail. Either owing to being abroad still, or due to inefficient advice,[3] he had not obtained, as he certainly could have, administration of the estates of his two dead brothers, so as to approach Chancery with this and claim a share of their holdings too. He therefore was simply awarded in 1823 his quarter share of the capital and cash interest in trust in Chancery, just as if John and Tom Keats were still alive, as indeed, for all the Court knew, they were, no affidavits having been sworn in any way to the contrary. The Court therefore ordered to George only his £800-odd capital and its £288 14s 5d interest.

The rest of the story of this part of the Keats inheritance is simply told. On 3 June 1824, Keats's sister Frances Mary

[1] See post, p. 51.
[2] P.R.O., C.33.710. f. 952.
[3] Fanny Keats blamed Abbey, who apparently held power of attorney for George's business affairs in England (KC, I, p. 298), but it is not certain that he acted for George in this matter.

(Fanny) came of age. She took the advice of two close friends of the poet, Charles Wentworth Dilke and James Rice. On 21 May 1825, she obtained the administration of the estates of her two dead brothers, John and Tom.[1] Armed with this, and with affidavits by witnesses who swore to the births and deaths of Tom and John, she applied to Chancery, the only one of the Keats children to do so at anything like the right time and in the right way. She received by the Orders of 3 June[2] and 20 December 1825,[3] not only her own capital and interest, but the capital and interest of John and Tom, with a slight deduction from the latter in favour of George. It has been wondered why she took the whole of John's share.[4] The explanation simply is that she had obtained administration of John's and Tom's estates, and George had not. All George was conceded—and he was lucky to get it—was just one-third of Tom's share of the original £1000 willed direct by John Jennings to the four Keats grandchildren. So when 'every penny', as Ralph Thomas said, had been accounted for from Chancery, Fanny Keats obtained the major part of what remained of the Keats inheritance there. It must be said that, although she does not seem to have been on very good terms with George, she acted with perfect propriety to him over this matter. On 31 May 1826, she informed him 'There is some property of yours in the Bank standing in my name, being your share of Tom's and John's property out of Chancery, after paying all debts. I cannot say the exact amount, but as Mr Rice intends sending you a statement I shall refer you to him.'[5] In fact, Rice, who was at that time in partnership with yet another friend of Keats, John Hamilton Reynolds, proved almost as dilatory as Chancery would have been in handing over George his money. Two years of misunderstanding and transatlantic correspondence were to take place before George seems finally to have received some sort of share of that part of the Keats inheritance which had lain so long in Chancery.[6]

[1] Principal Probate Registry, Administrations, 1825.
[2] P.R.O., C.33.735. ff. 1401 and 1402.
[3] P.R.O., C.33.744. f. 225.
[4] Hewlett, p. 376.
[5] KC, I, p. 298.
[6] KC, I, p. 315. Dilke seems to have arranged this.

Whatever he got, Fanny, who had her own financial ups and downs through the unwise speculations of her Spanish husband, was the only final gainer among all the Keats children. She had the advantage of outliving them all, and in her old age we find her enquiring through Ralph Thomas about something everyone else seems to have forgotten—the sum of £200-odd earmarked by Chancery for the Keats children's education but not applied owing to their mother's early death.[1] In this financial persistence, as perhaps in other things, she resembled her grandmother, whose legacy to the Keats children must now be considered so as to complete the story.

---

[1] Though Hewlett, p. 376, suggests Thomas may have obtained it for her, Fanny herself says he did not. 'Mr Thomas's Letters . . . are not favourable to me.' F.K.L., 6 October 1887.

Alice Jennings's Will

ONE major advantage of having made a thorough examination, for the first time, of the Chancery suit of Rawlings *v.* Jennings is that we can have a much more exact idea of Alice Jennings's own will and the inheritance that the Keats children might expect from that source. This again has been the subject of confused thinking and writing in many biographies and articles, though there is, in this instance, one basic cause why absolute accuracy cannot be attained. When Alice Jennings made her will on 31 July 1810, she referred in it to an 'Indenture or Deed' which she had signed the previous day; and this Indenture or Deed, which apparently gave the details of stock and money assigned in trust to the legatees, has been lost.

On the other hand, with the new knowledge of the precise stock and cash which she eventually received from Chancery, together with statements made later by Keats, his brother George and their close friends, it is now possible to come very near to the truth. This truth has been particularly obscured of recent years by the quite arbitrary assumption that one of the two trustees dealing with the Indenture, Richard Abbey, behaved fraudulently. This assumption has led to some extraordinary errors.[1]

The position is made relatively clear if we follow, without any confusing assumptions, the statement of two of Keats's friends, Charles Brown and Charles Wentworth Dilke, and of his own brother George. These are themselves sometimes obscured by the bitter quarrel that broke out between the first two about George's own financial dealings with Keats, but on the whole they agree remarkably well. To start with,

[1] See particularly Bate, and articles by Norman Kilgour, KSMB, XIII, pp. 24–27 and XIV, pp. 34–36.

there is an agreement between all three that though the basic legacy from their grandmother was equally divided between her four Keats grandchildren—John, George, Tom and Fanny—there was an additional special legacy for Fanny. Dilke, who had seen the figures but who was relying on memory when he made the statement, called it a special bequest of two or three hundred pounds. With the knowledge of what Alice Jennings received from John Jennings's estate, it can be seen what this may have been. Alice Jennings ultimately received, as we have seen, £8541 7s 7d capital and the clear residue of £267 10s 7d cash. The capital was tied up, according to her will,[1] in various trusts for the benefit of her grandchildren—including one, incidentally, for the Jennings grandchildren; but the amount of clear residue coincides so closely with the amount Dilke remembered that Fanny was left that it is extremely likely to have formed her special portion.

Fanny's additional cash portion apart, what was the stock willed in trust to each of the four Keats grandchildren? Here again, there is a remarkable consensus between the three statements, though the way they are put has caused some confusion. Brown said it was 'Property in the [Government] funds . . . £2000 to each of the brothers, and the remainder to the sister'.[2] Dilke, in correcting Brown's overestimate of the additional bequest to Fanny, said, 'The truth, I believe, was that the brothers were entitled to about £1500 each, or something less—& to Mrs Llanos[3] £1500 and two or three hundred more, a special bequest'. George says 'presuming 1500£ was the amount each of us possessed'.[4]

Now the apparent contradiction here is really not one at all. Brown was speaking of stock—specifically 'in the funds'— and the other two of its cash value when sold. George goes on to speak of the sale of his: 'the price of stocks advancing, the sale of mine produced 1600£'.[5] What each was left, then, was stock of approximately £2000, which at the time Mrs Jennings made her will stood at a price that would bring in about

[1] Principal Probate Registry, Effingham, 193.
[2] KC, II, p. 55.
[3] The married name of Fanny Keats.
[4] KC, I, p. 277.
[5] KC, I, p. 278.

£1500 each—something less, according to Dilke. Mrs Jennings, as we have seen earlier, held or was due to hold £8541 7s 7d stock, which had once been held by her husband, in the following holdings:

	£	s	d
East India Stock	500	0	0
Bank 3% Consol. annuities	4670	11	4
3% reduced annuities	2307	10	0
5% annuities 1797	1063	6	3

The cash value of this capital of just over £8541 would be high, largely because of the very high sale value of the smallest holding, the East India Stock of £500; but since we are told that each of the four grandchildren had £2000, making a total of £8000 stock, we must question whether this extra £500 East India Stock was ever willed to them. If we work out the cash value of all stock when Mrs Jennings made her will and its cash value when George cashed his share (4 June 1818), we can see that the statements of Brown, Dilke and George agree almost exactly *omitting* the East India Stock from the Keats children's inheritance. The value of each one's share at the time Mrs Jennings made her will would then be about £1470;[1] the value of George's share when he cashed it would be £1659 11s 6d.[2] This corresponds so closely with the '£1500 each, or something less' of Dilke, and 'the sale of mine produced 1600£' of George, that we can confidently say the East India Stock was not left to the Keats grandchildren. How it was left, in the absence of the trust provisions of the Deed, we cannot so confidently say; but it must be remembered that there was trust provision in the Deed for the children of Captain Jennings, that all this East India Stock had originally belonged, after his father's death, to him by the Order in Chancery of 29 July 1806, and that its absolute possession for his children had been petitioned by his widow in December 1809. It is therefore not at all beyond the bounds of probability that Alice Jennings returned this small but valuable capital in trust to her Jennings grandchildren.

Without it, the position of the Keats grandchildren becomes clear and explicable. Each had £2010 capital in 3 per cent

[1] G.M., 1810, Part 2, p. 200.
[2] G.M., 1818, Part 1, p. 576.

Consolidated, 3 per cent reduced, and 5 per cent Stock. These stocks fluctuated considerably in value since it was a time of war. At their grandmother's death late in 1814, the stocks were relatively low; they had, in fact, weakened slightly since she made her will, four years earlier, and had a potential cash value of only just over £1400. By the time John Keats came of age on 31 October 1816, stocks had been dramatically depressed by the panic of the Hundred Days in summer 1815. True, Napoleon had then been defeated at Waterloo, and the long war ended; but stocks had not recovered, and the post-war boom of 1817, from which George was to reap such benefit, had not yet begun. Even if Keats had kept all his capital intact, the cash value of his £2010 stock on his twenty-first birthday would only have been about £1230, a very low yield.[1]

This 'Even if' opens up one of the most disputed topics in all Keats biography. To put it briefly, George, in trying later to exculpate himself from the charge of having borrowed money from his brother, stated that Keats, in order to pay for his medical training and other expenses, had cashed and spent by the time of his twenty-first birthday, two-thirds of his capital. When he wrote this statement in a letter to Dilke of 10 April 1824, George was in a high condition of indignation and resentment at the way in which he felt he had been mis-represented 'by those reports so injurious to my honor—Brotherly affection—common honesty—which have so cruelly estranged others'. Unfortunately, his haste to come forward 'with the proof that I not only did not wrong my Brother in money concerns, but that I owed him little or nothing' was poured out in this letter with such breathless abbreviation and gap-jumping in thought and logic that it not only did his cause harm—though Dilke believed him—but obscured and confused some issues even for his contemporaries Brown and Dilke, let alone for later investigators. Yet this letter, with all its muddle and ellipsis, contains the truth, if we piece out carefully its most important portion:[2]

Now sum this up presuming 1500£ was the amount each of us possessed. Suppose with the *premium* to Mr Hammond
$£200$

---

[1] See Appendix V. [2] KC, I, pp. 277, 278.

£30 £50 50£
and *apprenticeship* fees, *dressership* and other *hospital* fees,
£20 20 £160 per an. Tom being with him
books and surgical *instruments*, and the *current* expenses between
the time of getting his indentures untill he was of age, nearly
4 years, he spent £1000, a most moderate calculation, he had
but 500£ left to lend 175£ which he informed me he did
and spend at least 200£ per annum untill I started to America,
almost 2 years, when I left him with nearly 300£. Up to that
time then I am probably £375 in advance. — I left England
three mos after I was of age with £1100; the price of stocks
advancing, the sale of mine produced 1600£, leaving 500£
and a present Mr Abbey made me the amount of which I do
not remember suppose 70 or 100£ to discharge about 100£
of debts and leave some means to my Brothers.

Removing some of the red herrings from this remarkably
excited account, written under the stress of indignant emotion,
three main statements are made, all of which have at one
time or another been misinterpreted or denied. They are

1. That John Keats, by the time he was of age on 31 October
1816 had sold, or had had sold for him by his trustees and
guardians, enough of his original capital to raise £1000 cash,
mostly spent on his medical training. This would involve a
gradual sale of about two-thirds of his capital of £2010.

2. That he cashed the remainder on his twenty-first birthday, living beyond his means and lending money, so that
when George went to America in June 1818, 'I left him with
nearly 300£'.

3. That the sale of George's capital, which had remained
untouched until his twenty-first birthday, produced £1600, of
which he took £1100 to America, 'leaving 500£ . . . to discharge about 100£ of debts and leave some means to my
Brothers'.

It must be admitted that since the way these facts were put
confused Brown and Dilke, there is no blame for the muddle
made of them by modern biographers, though they have
added some strange misconceptions of their own. To take the
first point, it has been hotly denied that Keats could have
spent anything like £1000 on his medical training.[1] This
denial is almost always based on the assumption that the
premium of two hundred pounds (guineas, George elsewhere

---

[1] Bate, p. 709, says 'We may exaggerate if we place it at a third of that.'

says) for Keats's apprenticeship to Thomas Hammond the surgeon is a ridiculous sum, and must be a complete exaggeration.[1] In actual fact, 200 guineas was the average premium for apprenticeship to a surgeon at that time. The Bindings Book of the Society of Apothecaries shows premiums that ranged from a nominal 5s (for a relative or a son of a friend) to £500.[2] Finally to clinch the matter, Hammond himself apprenticed his own son to a surgeon to whom he paid a premium of precisely 200 guineas.[3] On taking, within a matter of months, an apprentice himself, he naturally charged the same premium; one fee probably paid for the other.

Keats's trustees, therefore, had to sell part of his £2010 stock straight away to raise this premium, and this, assuming they sold some of the 3 per cent stock, would mean sacrificing capital of £310, leaving him from the start only £1700 stock. This is important as regards his annual interest for living expenses. A modern biographer[4] has criticized one of the Keats children's trustees, Abbey, for 'doling out to the children about £60 apiece as their annual income', but the criticism implied here is nonsense. It *was* their annual income; £2010 of the type of stocks he held for the children, equally apportioned, produces an annual income of about £65. John Keats, from the start of his apprenticeship, did not even have that; his capital having been reduced to £1700, his annual income was now only £55, ten pounds a year less than his brothers and sister.

The question then is, how much his further medical training and his living expenses compelled his trustees to sell out more and more of his capital. We may feel that George's total figure of £1000 cash, involving the sale of about £1150 more stock, after the initial sale of £310 for the 200-guinea premium, is a suspiciously round one; yet there is another witness to a comparable though not quite so large figure. A year after Keats's death, Brown called on Abbey and enquired about this exact point, the amount of cash spent on Keats's medical training; he reported 'Mr Abbey expatiated to me on the

[1] Lowell, I, 47; Bate, p. 30, n. even says 'Premiums were unusual.'
[2] G.L. Ms. 8207.
[3] Examination Books, Royal College of Surgeons of England.
[4] Bate, p. 710.

folly of his having left it [the profession of surgery] after he had spent £700 on it'.[1] The italics are Brown's; he accepts the figure as a possibility for the expenses of a medical training, and even admits later 'it is very possible he talked of £700 when he ought to have said £1000'. If Brown could accept these as credible figures for a five or six years' training there is no need to doubt George, especially remembering that each sale of capital would reduce Keats's annual income still further each time, and that the low value of stock at this period would give him comparatively little for each cash realization.

If Keats then, as now seems extremely probable, had, as his brother said, only £500 cash left of his legacy when he was twenty-one, what did he have left when George went to America a year and a half later? He had given up 'the profession of surgery' without ever, so far as one knows, taking any paid appointment. His capital was by now all cashed, or, if he had left any still in the funds, would only have produced a minute income. During this year and a half, with no earnings and no income except possibly a few pounds, he toured to the Isle of Wight, Margate, Canterbury and Hastings, living in lodgings at all of these, and writing the first book of *Endymion*; he shared lodgings with his brothers in Hampstead while writing Book Two; he journeyed to Oxford (though living free in College) to write Book Three, and made one excursion at least, to Stratford-upon-Avon; he completed Book Four at Box Hill, staying at an inn. He then spent a sociable winter in London, and the next spring in lodgings at Teignmouth. It was an expensive year and a half, whether or not, as George says, his habitual generosity also involved him in loans to friends; it would not be surprising if he cashed and spent something like £200, leaving £300 or probably less.

It is George's next statement about this sum remaining to Keats that has confused everyone, Brown, Dilke, and more modern commentators. No one has looked precisely at what he said in its exact context. George said, speaking of the time, June 1818, when he himself went to America, 'I left him with nearly 300£'. This has been universally taken to mean what

---

[1] Brown to Dilke, 6 September 1824, Keats House Collection. Printed in *The Everlasting Spell*, Joanna Richardson, Appendix I, p. 196.

it would mean if the word 'with' were removed: 'I left him nearly 300£', implying that George left John a present of £300 of his (George's) money. Brown, who accompanied George and John to the emigrant ship, hotly denies that John received any such present, which he, of course, would have known of at the time;[1] but the fact is that Brown, and everyone after him, mistook what George is saying here. In the context, which is a recital of the steady diminution of Keats's own cash resources, 'I left him *with* 300£' can only mean £300 *of his own*.

This is borne out by George's third statement, which has probably been more misinterpreted than any other. It is

I left England three mos after I was of age with £1100; the price of stocks advancing the sale of mine produced 1600£, leaving 500£ . . . to discharge about 100£ of debts and leave some means to my Brothers.

Endless muddle has been made out of this statement, which indeed is far from being crystal-clear. For one thing, it has been said George meant that the cash value of the stock he himself held had increased during his minority from £1100 to £1600; but even with the violent war and post-war fluctuations of the value of stock, which we have seen, the prices of the 3 per cent and 5 per cent stock involved do not support such figures as possible.

What George in fact means, once more in the context of his argument, is relatively plain, He held stock of £2010, whose cash value at the time of his grandmother's will was, as we have seen, £1470. When he encashed it on 4 June 1818, there had just been a year when Government stocks rose rapidly; therefore the sale of his stock brought him £1659 11s 6d, which he approximated as £1600. Now comes the vital point, which George, in his indignant excitement, has blurred: out of this £1600, he took £1100 only to America, and left behind £500 to discharge, as he says, about £100 of his debts 'and leave some means to my Brothers', John and Tom. This we know is true, since an exact documentary account, never before recognized as such, still exists of this £500.

This is the so-called Abbey Cocks 'Account' in the Keats

[1] *The Everlasting Spell*, Joanna Richardson, Appendix I, p. 203.

House Collection, Hampstead.[1] It is a statement of 'John K. in account with Abbey Cock', and on the credit side it begins with a credit to Keats 'By Cash' on 4 June 1818 of £500. This, together with an entry of £8 6s 1d interest at the end of the same year, are the only amounts on the credit side. The debit entries have been the subject of much mystification, as indeed has been the initial credit of £500, but there is no need for any mystery over either. The credit of £500 is identical with the £500 which George, as he said, left behind (three weeks before he sailed for America) to pay some of his debts and 'leave some means' for John and Tom. He put this cash to John's credit with the firm of tea-warehousemen of which their former trustee, Abbey, was senior partner; being abroad, he needed a business house at which to deposit it. The debit side shows first a few minor payments for tea, cocoa and sundries dating back to 1815; Abbey was simply settling for his firm some small and long-standing debts of the three brothers. The other debit withdrawals are all, with one exception, 'Cash' up to the time of Tom's death on 1 December 1818; that is, Keats was drawing for himself and Tom on the money George had left behind to provide 'some means to my Brothers'. After Tom's death, starting with an entry just eight days after it, all the debit entries are drawn to 'Himself', that is, John Keats, in whose name the account is headed. The one earlier exception which is neither 'Cash' nor 'Himself' is an entry on 9 July of a debit 'George Keats £30'. This has been said to be inexplicable, since George was on the high seas at that date, but it is in fact the entry which finally proves the whole nature of the account. It is a payment to discharge in George's absence some debt of his; this, as he himself says, had been part of his purpose in leaving behind this £500.

From this account, moreover, we can tell roughly what John owed George. The withdrawals to 'Cash', that is for John and Tom, total £220. Assuming that Tom, who was seriously ill most of this time, needed more—the largest withdrawal, on 20 June, almost certainly represents a payment of some of George's debts and some provision for Tom while Keats went off on a walking-tour—we may assume that John

[1] Facsimile in KSMB, XIV, p. 34. The accompanying text has several errors of fact and transcription. See Appendix VI.

drew to spend on himself about one-third of these, about £70. The withdrawals, all after Tom's death, to 'Himself'—that is, Keats himself—total £176, and there is a balance (not a withdrawal) of £46 7s 7d to his credit on 3 April 1819, which he presumably withdrew and spent later. He therefore drew for himself, at a very conservative estimate indeed, just under £300 of the money George left behind in England.

Tom died on 1 December 1818. In 1819 George got into financial difficulties in America, and returned at the end of the year to collect and convert to ready cash his share of Tom's capital, one-third. There can be no final certainty over this transaction, since we do not know whether Tom, like George, had kept his capital intact, or whether, like John, he had had some of it realized for him by his trustees, since he too never had a settled job. George says—to summarize his statement here—that Tom's capital was reduced so that it only raised £1100 cash. This is likely anyway, since there was a minor slump in stocks in 1819; even Keats himself noted 'that the Stocks are so very low'.[1] Each of the three surviving grandchildren at first took £100 of this cash, John remitting George's to him before he returned. Of the £800 remaining, Fanny kept her further £260 as a credit, but John only took a further £100. George took his own further £270 and the remaining £170 he took, he said, from John's share. Even if we assume that Tom's estate was intact, and that George underestimated its value, which at the then market price would be between £1300 and £1400, George could not have gone off with more than £300 of John's share, exactly equalling what John had spent previously of George's own money, as shown by the Abbey-Cocks document. In fact, the highest probability seems to be that at Christmas 1819 the accounts of these two surviving brothers were just about even, and that there was no financial reason for any grievance or quarrel. before Keats's death or posthumously.

In the affairs of all three Keats brothers, it will be now observed, there is no hint of the duplicity or even fraud of which their trustee Abbey has been accused: quite the reverse. The story of the £2010 capital left in his hands for each boy may be summarized. For John, he seems to have realized the

[1] Letters, II, p. 229. See also Appendix V.

larger part to pay for his medical education and some living expenses during his minority. John, unemployed as far as earning was concerned, never acquired the means to put back this capital, and spent the balance of the cash after he was twenty-one. For George, who had a position in his own warehouse, he kept intact the capital in its original holdings, so that at George's coming-of-age it realized nearly £200 more than might have been expected. Two-thirds of Tom's capital, after the latter's death, he realized for John and George. He was reluctant to do this at first, thinking that as trustee for her he should perhaps wait till the third sharer, Fanny, became of age. Keats dismissed this impatiently as 'all a Bam'—i.e. a put-up job[1]—but there may very well have been something to this effect in the Indenture or Deed attached to their grandmother's will. At all events Abbey did eventually release their shares to both John and George. George took the larger part of this in what now seems a legitimate settlement of John's debt to him.

The fact is that, in a kind of witch-hunt after Abbey, many people have read back his dishonest conduct after Keats's death to Fanny Keats—which is undoubted—into his dealings with John Keats and the two other boys during Keats's lifetime. There is no doubt that he attempted to swindle Fanny; but even she, injured as she was, and calling Abbey roundly 'that consummate villain' never made the mistake of thinking that he had done anything dishonest to her brothers. She is clear that Abbey did not rob the Keats boys nor interfere with their inheritance since he himself until the early 1820s 'had no occasion to rob being at the time . . . possessed of considerable property'.[2] What quite simply seems to have happened was that Abbey was involved in the speculative trade boom of 1822-25, and caught, like so many others, in the panic of 1825.[3] Fanny Keats was twenty-one on 3 June 1824. The value of stock was at the peak of the boom at that date, and her £2010 stock would be worth about £1927 cash.[4] In addition, she had her one-third share of whatever

[1] Letters, II, p. 40.
[2] KC, I, p. 298.
[3] *The Growth and Fluctuation of the British Economy, 1790-1850*, Gayer, Rostow and Schwartz, I, pp. 190, 191.
[4] G.M., 1824, Vol. I, p. 576. See Appendix V.

stock or cash Tom had left, perhaps amounting to £500, and her special legacy of two or three hundred pounds left her by her grandmother from the residue of her grandfather's estate. These figures seem approximately confirmed by the fact that Abbey was eventually sued, by Dilke and Rice, for a total of £2905 18s.[1] This sum, or nearly, was what he should have handed over to her on her twenty-first birthday. He did not, and 'a twelvemonth's urgings and evasions'[2] took place. Abbey was not a pleasant man personally, if we are to judge by his attitude to Keats. He had seen more of Fanny than of the other Keats children, and familiarity had bred the kind of contempt through which he was perhaps able in some way to justify his wrong-dealing to himself. He may also have gambled on Fanny's mistaken idea, which she maintained to the end of her life obstinately and in the face of baptismal records, that she had been born not in 1803 but in 1804, thus giving him an extra year to manipulate and then perhaps pay back her capital. As it was, he was caught out; as she had done over the Chancery fund, she called in Dilke and Rice, Keats's friends, who interested themselves in her situation and obtained her inheritance from Abbey, forcing him in the process to mortgage his property. It is not certain, though, that they obtained the whole of this part of her inheritance. Dilke only records that they obtained £1893 10s 3d 3 per cent stock, which might represent her 3 per cent stock and a share of Tom's.[3] Abbey had probably realized the 5 per cent stock when that was converted and reissued in 1822.

So the distribution of the rich estate of John Jennings ended, as it had begun, in litigation. Of all the litigants, in person or by proxy, it may be thought that John Keats was among the most unfortunate. Through his reticence, we do not know what impression he carried from his early childhood about his family background; but the known circumstances of his grandfather must have left a sense of ease and prosperous living. We get a hint of this in the story that his mother would have liked to have sent him and his brothers to school at

[1] KSMB, V, pp. 26–31. 'New Light on Mr Abbey', Joanna Richardson.
[2] MLPKC, p. 31.
[3] Ralph Thomas Ms. Dilke, not trusting her husband, put all this stock in trust in Chancery so that she only received interest for the rest of her life. F.K.L.

Harrow. This sense of prosperity seems to have formed a background to his life, which made it even more irritating and inexplicable to him when its actual achievement always seemed to evade him. Throughout his letters there is a sense of some fate or ill-luck always working in some undefined way against him. In one of the very last, he burst out, 'O, that something fortunate had ever happened to me or my brothers!'[1] Yet it was not blind or malignant fate but the operations of various kinds of human conduct, his own included, that produced this frustrating result. Now that we at last know most of the strictly material facts, we can conclude by examining this conduct in the light of the story of the Keats inheritance.

[1] Letters, II, p. 352.

Epilogue

THE story of the Keats inheritance may appear at one level as a middle-class Greek tragedy. The head of a family, John Jennings acquires considerable wealth. No sooner is he in his grave than his riches are disputed by his family, which contains in itself a hereditary tendency to early death. Their legal action delays the enjoyment of his wealth until their hereditary weakness cuts them off. One of this family is a genius. His life and work is entangled in this web before he is even aware of it, and he dies before he realizes he is entitled to part of a fortune.

Another way of looking at it is from the point of view of human fallibility and error. John Jennings was generous, and what one of his grandsons called 'gullable'.[1] He tried, in disposing of his wealth, to please everyone, and pleased no one. His temperament had its counterpart in the impetuosity with which his descendants rushed to law to settle their claims. When this generous strain reached his grandson, the poet, it showed itself in a carelessness about material affairs which Keats himself often admitted, and a perpetual feeling that something would turn up without effort on his part. It led to his failing to get the benefit of his inheritance, neglecting to apply for a part of it, and spending most of the rest on a profession which he did not eventually follow.

Yet another way of regarding the story is from a purely financial and economic angle.[2] The larger part of John Jennings's fortune was in Government stock. He died in the middle of a drastic and long war, when the fate of the country stood in the balance, and when Government stock stood at an extremely low quotation. Those of his descendants who could

---

[1] KC, I, p. 314.
[2] Appendix V.

refrain from cashing the stock until war ended, and could wait for the post-war boom, would do well out of it. John Keats was unlucky enough to have an expensive apprenticeship to pay for entirely in the war period, and therefore his stock had to be realized at disadvantageous terms. If, like his brother George and sister Fanny, he had been able to keep it intact until peacetime, he would have had a richer inheritance.

All these legitimate ways of regarding the story have been previously confused by the penchant of Anglo-Saxon writers for trying to find a villain to blame; first, Keats's stepfather has been pressed into this role, and when he leaves the scene, Keats's guardian has been cast to take up the part. When the facts are known, the best summary of the situation may be found in the words of another poet:

> In tragic life, God wot,
> No villain need be! Passions spin the plot:
> We are betrayed by what is false within.

For the importance of the whole story of the Keats inheritance is how it affected Keats as a poet. To begin with, it seems clear that in early childhood, John Jennings's wealth gave Keats a feeling of security and affluence. His mother, who treated John in particular of all her children with 'prodigallity and doting fondness',[1] had been brought up in a well-to-do atmosphere with no lack of money. We do not know quite how much this persisted after her marriages; indeed, a case could be made for the supposition that John Jennings retained so much capital at his death partly because he had made no marriage settlements during life on his daughter; this might account for the startling difference between his estate and that of his brother-in-law Sweetingburgh, a man in a comparable sphere of life, who may have settled much on his two married daughters. Whatever the arrangement, Frances came from a prosperous background and no doubt brought up her children in an atmosphere of prosperity. Keats began in a world free from material cares.

Then there was a dramatic change in his life. This has always been associated solely with his father's death and his mother's speedy remarriage; but the effect of this we simply

[1] KC, I, p. 314.

do not know. What we do know now is that the family litigation over his grandfather's will split this family security from
top to bottom—mother against uncle, mother against grandmother, her own mother. For a volatile and observant boy,
this may have been far more world-shaking than his mother's
remarriage. The quotation from *Hamlet*, 'But two months dead'
has been applied aptly to that event;[1] but another quotation
from Keats's loved *Troilus and Cressida* could be applied to the
change wrought by the lawsuit: 'This is and is not Cressid'.
The people he had known to love and trust, a doting mother,
a hero uncle, a 'Granny-good' suddenly appeared as different
people, as hostile opponents, with whom inevitably sides had
to be taken. Having to set up home not with their mother but
with their grandmother was only part of an even more funda-
mental split in the whole of family life. It explains Keats's
curious sense of isolation, which lasted all through his life, so
that he could say of his most intimate friends 'they do not
know me'. It explains why he seems to have no relations in
the outside world. At a blow, a barrier falls between him and
his three young Jennings cousins; it was so complete that
they never appear in his letters, and when the daughter of
one wrote a family memoir long after Keats's fame was estab-
lished, she never mentioned that they were related to the poet.[2]

These events of the Keats inheritance may certainly have
been the forcing-ground of Keats as a poet. Great security
followed by a reversal may well have worked in this way; in
particular, the inevitability of death, the theme of nearly all
his great poems, was brought dramatically to his notice. No
sooner did one of these near relatives seem to be on the point
of prosperity and stable life than death removed him or her.
He appears to work through all this, and enter into life himself unmaimed; but much of this early experience remained
with him. The contrasts of fortune he had learned left their
counterparts in the alternations of his own nature between
intense gaiety and joy and moods of deep depression, the
'hypocondriasm' of which his nearest brother spoke,[3] and
which he himself admitted.

1 Ward, p. 11.
2 KSMB, XIV, p. 37.
3 KC, I, p. 284.

So far, one can hardly quarrel with the Keats inheritance if one wants the stock of English poetry increased; but in its later working-out, it may have hindered more than it benefited that poetry and even have deprived us of some. Admittedly, the actual money he inherited gave him, if not the 'ten years' he required for poetic fulfilment, at least the four or five he used so magnificently, when he did not need to be employed in anything but the practice of a poet; but he could, if he had known, have had more to spend with a like creative prodigality. If he could have had this considerable extra portion—for, as we have seen, the unclaimed Chancery fund amounted to precisely two-sevenths of his total potential fortune—he might have been encouraged to be more prudent in a worldly sense and preserve himself longer and for later work; it might even have postponed the progress of his fatal disease.

One cannot dogmatize about the effects of outside circumstances on tuberculosis, but it seems that material worry can at any rate be a quickening factor. In considering Keats's illness, we must remember that his brother George, the only boy apparently to resist the 'family disease', went down with it suddenly in his forties after suffering severe financial reverse and anxiety. The fatal process started by Keats's mother may be thought of in these terms. By introducing financial stress into a family that had hitherto known none, she may well have killed prematurely first her brother, then herself, and then at long range and posthumously her poet son. Leigh Hunt wrote at random when he said of her: 'his mother, who was a lively woman, passionately fond of amusement, is supposed to have hastened her death by too great an inattention to hours and seasons. Perhaps she hastened that of her son.'[1] His casual remarks, derived probably at second-hand through Keats's publisher, may contain a truth that he could not have known. It seems certain that the Keats inheritance both helped to give us and to deprive us of great poetry. There is no measure in such matters of its exact effect. We can only contemplate the facts and form our own conclusions.

---

[1] Leigh Hunt, *Lord Byron and Some of his Contemporaries*, 1828, p. 247.

Bill of Complaint, 6 April 1805

To the Right Honorable John Lord Eldon Baron Eldon of Eldon in the County Palatine of Durham Lord High Chancellor of Great Britain. Humbly complaining shew unto your Lordship your Orator and Oratrix William Rawlings of Moorgate in the City of London Stable Keeper and Frances his wife formerly Frances Jennings Spinster and late Frances Keates widow that John Jennings late of Ponders End in the parish of Enfield in the county of Middlesex your Oratrixs late father deceased being possessed of a large personal Estate duly made and published his last Will and Testament in writing bearing date the first day of February one thousand eight hundred and five and thereby after directing his just debts should be paid amongst other things gave and bequeathed as follows "I give and bequeath unto my wife Alice Jennings two hundred pounds per year being part of the monies I now have in Bank Security intirely for her own use and benefit together with all my household furniture and effects of what nature or kind soever that I may be possessed of at the time of my decease I give and bequeath unto my son Midgley John Jennings Two thousand pounds that I have in East India Stock and one thousand nine hundred pounds being part of the monies that I have in Bank Security called the new fives for his use during his natural life and if he should die without issue I then give and bequeath to his widow if living at the time of his decease the sum of five hundred pounds and the remaining part to return to my family I give and bequeath to my daughter Frances Rawlins wife of William Rawlins fifty pounds per year during her natural life and after her decease the same to be equally divided amongst my grandchildren sons and daughters of the said Frances Rawlins (that is to say) John Keats George Keats Thomas Keats and Frances Keats sons and daughter of the late Thomas Keats and the said Testator after giving divers pecuniary legacies and annuities to the said Grandchildren and to certain persons in the said Will named appointed Charles Danvers of Upper Thames Street London and the said Testator's son the said Midgley John Jennings Executors and his wife Alice Jennings Executrix of his said Will as in or by the said Will or the Probate thereof and to which your Orator and Oratrix crave leave to refer relation being thereto had will more fully appear And your Orator and Oratrix further shew that the said Testator departed this life on or about the Eighth day of March last without altering or revoking his said Will leaving the said Alice Jennings his wife and two children namely your Oratrix Frances Rawlings and the said Midgley John Jennings his only children him surviving and shortly after the said Testator's death the said Midgley John Jennings one of the Executors and Alice Jennings the Widow the Executrix in the said Will named duly proved the same in the prerogative Court of the Archbishop of Canterbury and took upon themselves the Execution thereof but the said Charles Danvers hath not yet proved the said Will nor at all acted in the trusts thereof nor possessed nor received any part of the said Testator's effects And your Orator and Oratrix shew that the said Midgley John Jennings and the said Alice Jennings or one of them hath possessed the said Testator's personal Estate and Effects and much more than sufficient to answer and satisfy the Testator's just debts funeral expenses annuities and legacies with a surplus remaining And your Orator and Oratrix shew that the said Testator was not possessed of any long annuities but he was possessed of twenty four pounds per Annum short annuities standing in his name in the Bank Books and the said Testator was not only possessed of such sum of Two thousand pounds East India Stock and one thousand nine hundred pounds five per cent annuities in the Will mentioned but was possessed also of other stocks and government funds and India stock to a considerable amount and other securities for money and other personal Estate to a considerable amount and which hath been possessed by his said Executors and Executrix or one of them And your Orator and Oratrix shew that the said Alice Jennings the Widow and your Oratrix Frances Rawlings and the said Midgley John Jennings are the only next of Kin of the said Testator And your Orator and Oratrix shew that the Testator not having bequeathed nor disposed of the residue of his personal Estate died intestate with respect thereto and the same belongs to your Orator and Oratrix in right of your oratrix Frances Rawlings and to the said Alice Jennings and the said Midgley John Jennings as his next of Kin and ought to be paid to and equally divided amongst them according to the Statute of Distribution and your oratrix Frances Rawlings or your orator William Rawlings in her right is intitled to have and receive the said annuity bequeathed to her as aforesaid secured and paid to her for her life and to have a sufficient sum of money invested and set apart to answer the same and also to have an account of the Testators personal Estate and to have the same ascertained and applied as aforesaid and for that purpose your Orator and Oratrix have frequently applied to the said

Midgley John Jennings and Alice Jennings the Executor and
Executrix and requested them to secure and pay the said Annuity
of fifty pounds to your Orator and Oratrix and to render such
account as aforesaid and your Orator and Oratrix hoped they
would have complied with such reasonable request as in Justice
and Equity they ought to do But now so it may please your Lordship the said Midgley John Jennings and Alice Jennings combining
with the said Charles Danvers and other persons to your Orator
and Oratrix unknown whose names when discovered they pray
they may insert herein as parties Defendants refuse to render any
such account of the said personal Estate sometimes pretending that
the said Testator did not make any such Will and at other times
they admit that the said Testator made such will and that they
have proved the same and possessed themselves of all his personal
estate but then they pretend that the same was very small and
inconsiderable and not near sufficient to pay and satisfy all the
said Testators just debts legacies and funeral expences and that
they have applied and disposed of the same towards satisfaction
thereof and at the same time the said Confederates do respectively
refuse to set forth and discover what such personal Estate was or
the particulars whereof the same consisted or the value thereof or
how much thereof they have applied and to whom and for what
paid or what is become thereof particularly whereas your Orator
and Oratrix charge the truth to be that the said Testator died
possessed of such or some considerable personal Estate to the full
value aforesaid and which was much more than would pay all his
the said Testators just debts legacies and funeral expenses and the
said Confederates and particularly the said Alice Jennings and
Midgley John Jennings or one of them have possessed and converted the same to their own uses without making any satisfaction
to your Orator and Oratrix for the said Annuity of fifty pounds so
given to your Oratrix for her life as aforesaid and the said Confederates alledge and pretend that your Orator and Oratrix have
no right to any account of or interest in the residue of the Testators
Estate and the said Alice Jennings insists that she is intitled not
only to the sum of Two hundred pounds a year for her life but
that she is intitled absolutely to as much stock as will produce two
hundred pounds a year and she also insists that the said Testator
did dispose of the residue and that he did not die intestate with
respect thereto and she claims to be intitled to the whole residue
of the said Testators Estate and effects after payment of the debts
legacies and annuities given by his said Will and the said confederate Alice Jennings at other times pretends and the said
Midgley John Jennings insists that if the said Testator did not dispose of such residue and in case the said Alice is not intitled to the
whole of such residue that the same belongs to the said confederates

as Executors and Executrix of the said Will the said Testator having given unequal legacies to the said Alice Jennings and Midgley John Jennings and no legacy at all to the said Confederate Charles Danvers and therefore that they are intitled to such undisposed residue And the said Midgley John Jennings also alledges and insists that he is not only intitled to the said sum of Two thousand pounds East India Stock and one thousand nine hundred pounds five per cent annuities for his life but that in case he should die leaving issue he or his said issue will be intitled absolutely thereto Whereas your Orator and Oratrix charge the contrary of all such pretences to be true and that the said Confederate Alice Jennings under the true construction of the said Will is only intitled to two hundred pounds a year for her life and that she is not intitled to the whole of the residue of the Testators estate but that the same is undisposed of and that the said Testator died intestate with respect thereto and your Orator and Oratrix charge that upon the death of the said Midgley John Jennings without issue the said two thousand pounds East India Stock and one thousand nine hundred pounds five per cent Bank annuities will fall into and become part of the residue of the said Testators personal Estate and that the confederates the Executors are not intitled to such undisposed residue or any part thereof but that the same will belong to your Orator and Oratrix in right of your Oratrix and to the other next of kin of the said Testator under the Statute of Distributions and under the true construction of the said Will the said Testator never intended that the said Confederates the Executors and Executrix should take the said residue for their own benefit but that the same should go to his family and next of kin and that the said confederates the Executors are Trustees thereof for the said Testators next of kin nevertheless under such or the like pretences the said Confederates withhold and refuse to come to any account with your Orator and Oratrix respecting the matters aforesaid and the said Charles Danvers alledges that he has not proved the said Will and that he does not intend to do so yet he claims as such Executor to be intitled to a share of the residue of the said Testators personal Estate All which actings pretences and doings of the said Confederates are contrary to Equity and good conscience and tend to the manifest injury and oppression of your Orator and Oratrix In consideration whereof, and for that your Orator is remediless in the premises at and by the strict rules of Common Law and is only relievable in a Court of Equity where matters of this nature are properly cognizable To the End therefore that the said Midgley John Jennings Alice Jennings and Charles Danvers and the rest of the confederates when discovered may respectively full true direct and perfect answer make upon their respective corporal oaths according to the best of their respective

knowledge remembrance information and belief to all and singular
the matters and charges aforesaid as fully in every respect as if the
same were here again repeated and they thereunto particularly
interrogated and more especially that they may respectively set
forth and discover according to the best of their knowledge remembrance information and belief whether the said Testator John
Jennings did not duly make and execute such last Will and Testament in writing of such date and to such purport and effect as
aforesaid and thereby bequeathed such legacy or annuity of fifty
pounds as aforesaid to your Oratrix or any other or what last Will
of any other and what like and to any other and what purport
and effect particularly and that they may produce the same or the
probate thereof to this Honorable Court as often as there shall be
occasion and whether by such Will or any other and what Will the
said Testator did not appoint the Confederates Executors and
Executrix or any other and what Executors by name and when the
said Testator died and whether he revoked or altered the said
Will before his death and when and before whom and in what
manner And whether the said Confederates or one or which of
them proved the said Will and when and in what Court and that
they may respectively set forth whether the said Testator did not
leave your Oratrix and the said confederate Midgley John Jennings
his only children and the said Alice his widow and whether your
Oratrix and the said Confederates Midgley John Jennings and the
said Alice are not the only next of kin of the said Testator or who
else are And whether your Orator and Oratrix did not intermarry
in the life time of the Testator And whether your Orator and
Oratrix are not intitled to such Annuity of fifty pounds as aforesaid
And whether your Orator and Oratrix have not applied to them
the said Confederates to account for and set forth an account of the
Testators personal Estate and to ascertain the residue thereof and to
have the same paid or secured to be paid for the benefit of your
Orator and Oratrix or to that effect and whether the said Confederates
or one or which of them refused or neglected to comply with such
your Orators and Oratrixs requests and for what reasons respectively and whether such refusal is grounded upon the pretences
hereinbefore charged or any and which of them or any other and
what pretences particularly and that the said Confederates may
admit assets of the said Testator to come to their hands sufficient
to satisfy your Oratrix's said annuity of fifty pounds so given to
her for her life as aforesaid and that they may also set forth a particular account of the personal estate goods and effects of which the
said Testator died possessed or intitled unto and the particulars
whereof the same consisted and the nature kinds and values thereof
and how and in what manner and how much thereof they have
applied in discharge of his the said Testators debts legacies and

funeral expences and to whom and for what purpose and what is become thereof particularly and whether the said Testator did not die possessed of personal estate goods and effects to the value of Twelve thousand Pounds or what other value and whether the same was not much more than would pay all his just debts legacies and funeral expences and if not why not and that they may also set forth a just and true account of all such debts and sums of money as were really due and owing by and from the said Testator at the time of his death and to whom by name and upon what security or securities and how and on what account such debts were respectively contracted and which of them now remain unpaid and unsatisfied And whether the said Testator did not die intestate with respect to the residue of his personal Estate or how otherwise or how and in what manner he disposed of the same and to whom and whether the same ought not to be divided and distributed amongst his next of kin and if not why not and whether the said Executors are not Trustees of such undisposed residue for your Oratrix and the other next of kin and if not why not And whether the said Confederates do not claim to be intitled to the same residue and such other or some and what interest in the said Testators said Estate and how they respectively make out the same and that an account may be taken by and under a Decree of this Honorable Court of all and singular the personal Estate and Effects of which the said Testator died possessed or intitled unto and which hath come to the hands possession or power of the said Defendants Midgley John Jennings Alice Jennings and Charles Danvers the Executors or any person for their own or either of their use and that they may answer and pay the same respectively and that the said Testators said personal estate may be applied in payment of the Testators debts funeral expences and legacies in a course of Administration and that your Oratrixs said annuity of fifty pounds may be secured and paid to your Orator and Oratrix in right of and during the life of your Oratrix and that a proper sum of money may be invested in the name of the Accountant General of this Court for answering the same and that it may be declared that the said sum of Two thousand pounds East India Stock and one thousand nine hundred pounds five per cent Bank annuities given by the said Testators Will to the said Midgley John Jennings for his life will upon his death fall into and become part of the residue of the Testators personal Estate and that the said residue of the said personal Estate may be ascertained and that it may be declared that the same is undisposed of and that the Defendants the Executors are and ought to be considered and declared Trustees for your Oratrix and other the Testators next of kin and that the same ought to be distributed and divided equally between your Oratrix Frances Rawlings and your Orator in her

right and the said Defendants Midgley John Jennings and Alice
Jennings as the only next of kin of the said Testator and that the
same may be paid to them accordingly and that all necessary and
proper directions may be given for the purposes aforesaid And
that your Orator and Oratrix may have such other and further
relief in the premises as the nature of the case may require and as
to your Lordship may seem meet May it please your Lordship to
grant unto your orator and oratrix his Majesty's most gracious
Writ or Writs of Subpoena to be directed to them and to each of
them the said Midgley John Jennings Alice Jennings and Charles
Danvers thereby commanding them and each of them at a certain
day and under a certain pain therein to be limited personally to
be and appear before your Lordship in this Honorable Court and
then and there upon their and each of their corporal oaths to
answer all and singular the premises and further to stand and
abide by such further order and direction and decree of this
Honorable Court therein as to your Lordship shall seem meet

And your Orator and Oratrix shall ever pray &c.

Shaddick[1]   Jas Trower[2]

[1] Endorsed by Defendants' Clerk in Court.
[2] Plaintiffs' Counsel.

The several Answer of Midgley John Jennings, 6 April 1805

The several Answer of Midgley John Jennings one of the Defendants to the Bill of Complaint of William Rawlings and Frances his wife complainants. This Defendant saving to himself all benefit of exception to the Complainants said bill of complaint for answer thereto or so much thereof as is material for him to answer Answereth and saith he admits it to be true that John Jennings in the bill named did make and publish his last will and testament in writing of such date and to such purport and effect as in the Complainants bill is mentioned and set forth as far as the same is therein mentioned and set forth and that he appointed this Defendant and Alice his (the Testator's) wife and Charles Danvers—executors and executrix thereof but for greater certainty this Defendant refers to the said will or probate thereof when produced And this Defendant admits that the said Testator departed this life at or about the time in the bill mentioned without altering or revoking his said will leaving the said Alice his wife and the Complainant Frances the wife of the Complainant William Rawlings and this Defendant his only children and also his only next of Kin as in the bill mentioned And this Defendant admits that the said Alice Jennings and this Defendant alone proved the said will in the prerogative Court of the Archbishop of Canterbury and that they have taken upon themselves the execution thereof and that the said Charles Danvers hath never proved the same or possessed any part of the Testators assets or in any manner acted in the trusts of the said will but hath declined so to do and this Defendant admits that he and the said Alice Jennings have possessed some part of the Testators estate and effects and that the said Testator was entitled to certain stocks and funds that is to say one thousand pounds East India Stock six thousand four hundred and ninety three pounds six shillings three per cent consolidated Bank annuities two thousand three hundred and seven pounds ten shillings three per cent reduced Bank annuities two thousand and thirteen pounds six shillings and three pence five per cent one thousand seven hundred and ninety seven and twenty four pounds per annum short annuities and to some other personal estate but to what amounts in particular this Defendant cannot at present set forth but this Defendant submits to set forth and account for the same and for all such parts thereof as this Defendant hath already received or may hereafter receive in such manner as this Honourable Court may direct And this Defendant saith he believes that the complainants may be entitled to such annuity or legacy of fifty pounds per annum during the life of the said Complainant Frances Rawlings and this Defendant saith he doth claim to be entitled to have and receive the interest and dividends of the said capital sum of one thousand pounds East India Stock and one thousand nine hundred pounds five per cent Bank annuities give him by the said will for his life and this Defendant submits to the Judgment of this Honourable Court whether the capital thereof will upon the death of this Defendant without issue sink into the residue of the Testators personal estate or not and whether on the Death of this Defendant leaving issue surviving him the said capital will or will not belong and become payable to and divisible between such issue but this Defendant submits and insists that the said Alice Jennings is not entitled to the capital of the stock which will produce two hundred per annum but only to the sum of two hundred pounds per annum for her life And this Defendant denies that it was the Testators intention that this Defendant and his Co-executors should be considered or that they ought to be considered Trustees for the Complainant and others the Testators next of Kin on the contrary this Defendant claims as one of the said executors to be entitled to and to have a share of all such part of the said residue of the Testators estate as will appear not to be disposed of otherwise by his will and that the same when ascertained ought to be paid and divided between and amongst this Defendant and his said co-executors but in case the Court shall be of a contrary opinion then this Defendant claims to be entitled to a distributive part of such residue as one of the next of Kin of the said Testator and this Defendant denies all unlawful combination and confederacy in and by the said bill charged against him without this that there is any other matter or thing in the Complainants said bill of complaint contained material or effectual in the law for this Defendant to make answer unto and not herein and hereby well and sufficiently answered unto con-fessed or avoided traversed or denied is true to the knowledge of him this Defendant All which matters and things this Defendant is ready to aver maintain and prove as this Honourable Court shall award And therefore humbly prays to be hence dismissed with his reasonable costs and charges by him about his suit in this behalf most wrongfully sustained.

The joint and several Answer of Alice Jennings and Charles Danvers, 9 April 1805

The joint and several Answer of Alice Jennings Widow and Charles Danvers two of the Defendants to the bill of Complaint of William Rawlings and Frances his wife Complainants—
These Defendants reserving to themselves all Benefit of Exception to the Complainants said bill of Complaint for Answer thereto or so much thereof as is material for them to answer each answering for himself and herself and not the one for the other of them severally answer and say they admit it to be true that John Jennings the Testator in the bill mentioned duly made and published his last will and Testament in writing of such date and to such purport and effect as in the Bill set forth and thereby gave to his wife this Defendant Alice Jennings two hundred pounds per year being part of the monies he then had in bank security entirely for her own use and benefit together with all his household furniture and effects of what nature or kind soever that he might be possessed of at the time of his decease and the said Testator after giving such Legacies and bequests as in the bill mentioned appointed these Defendants and Midgley John Jennings his son Executors and Executrix of his said will as in and by the said Will or the probate thereof when produced will more fully appear And these Defendants admit that the said Testator departed this life at or about the time in the bill mentioned without altering or revoking his said Will leaving this Defendant Alice his Widow and leaving the said Midgley John Jennings and the Complainant Frances the wife of the Complainant William Rawlings his only children and next of kin him surviving And these Defendants admit that this Defendant Alice Jennings and the said Defendant Midgley John Jennings duly proved the said will in the proper Eccleastical Court and took upon themselves the burthen of the execution thereof and possessed themselves of the Testators personal Estate and Effects but this Defendant Charles Danvers saith and this Defendant Alice Jennings admits the same to be true that he hath never proved the said will nor doth he ever intend to prove the same nor hath

he possessed any part of the said Testators Estate or effects nor in
any manner acted or intermeddled in the said Testators Affairs or
concerns And this Defendant Alice Jennings saith that the said
Testator was entitled at the time of his Death to the several sums
of money following standing in the public funds in his name that
is to say one thousand pounds East India Stock Six thousand four
hundred and ninety three pounds six shillings three per cent consolidated Bank Annuities two thousand three hundred and seven
pounds ten shillings three per cent Reduced Bank Annuities two
thousand and thirteen pounds six shillings and three pence five per
cent one thousand seven hundred and ninety seven and twenty
four pounds Pr annums Short Annuities and other personal Estate
but to what amount in particular this Defendant doth not know
nor can set forth as to her belief save as herein is mentioned but
this Defendant Alice Jennings submits to set forth and account for
the same and all such parts thereof as she hath already received
or may hereafter receive in such manner as this Honourable Court
shall direct And these Defendants say they believe the Complainants intermarried together as mentioned in the said bill and
that the complainants in right of the said Complainant Frances
Rawlings may be entitled to such Annuity of fifty pounds her for life
as in the bill mentioned And these Defendants believe the Defendant
Midgley John Jennings is entitled to the interests and dividends
of two thousand pounds East India Stock and one thousand nine
hundred pounds Bank five per cent Annuities for his life and that
upon his Death the same will sink into and become part of the
Testators personal Estate And this Defendant Alice Jennings
submits that she is not only entitled to the sum of two hundred
pounds per annum for life but also to the capital of the Stock which
will produce the said annual sum of two hundred pounds absolutely
and for her own use and disposal And this Defendant Alice Jennings
submits that under the bequest of all the Testators Effects of what
nature or kind soever in the Will mentioned this Defendant is
entitled to all the said Testators personal effects not otherwise
disposed of by his said Will but in case it shall appear that any
part of the said Estate and effects was undisposed of then this
Defendant Alice Jennings insists that the same belong to this
Defendant and the said Midgley John Jennings and this Defendant
Charles Danvers as Executors of his said Will and that it was not
the intention of the Testator that the same should go to his next
of kin and that these defendants and the other Executor are not
nor ought to be considered Trustees for the next of kin But this
Defendant Alice Jennings saith that if the Court should be of a
different opinion then this Defendant Alice Jennings claims to be
entitled as the Testators Widow and one of his next of kin under
the statute to her distributive part or share of all such undisposed

Residue of the said personal Estate and effects And this Defendant Charles Danvers for himself saith that he disclaims all right or interest whatever of in or to the said Testators Estate or Effects which he may or can have or claim as Executor or otherwise howsoever and claims to be discharged from all the trusts of the said Will and from intermeddling or acting therein And these Defendants deny all unlawful combination in and by the said Bill charged against them without this that there is any other matter or thing in the Complainants said bill of Complaint contained material or effectual in the law for these Defendants to make answer unto and not herein and hereby well and sufficiently answered unto confessed or avoided traversed or denied is true to the knowledge of them these Defendants All which matters and things these Defendants are ready to aver maintain and prove as this Honourable Court shall award and therefore humbly prays to be hence dismissed with their reasonable costs and charges by them about their suit in this behalf most wrongfully sustained.

The Reply and Account of Midgley John Jennings, 28 December 1805

William Rawlings and Frances Rawlings Plaintiffs

and

Midgley John Jennings, Alice Jennings and Charles Danvers Defendants

The Several Answer of the Defendant Midgley John Jennings to an Interrogatory exhibited on the behalf of the above named Plaintiffs before Alexander Popham Esquire one of the Masters of this Court for the examination of the said Defendants Midgley John Jennings and Alice Jennings pursuant to the Decree made on the hearing of this cause bearing date the eighth day of May one thousand eight hundred and five To this Interrogatory this Defendant Midgley John Jennings saith that to the best of his knowledge remembrance information and belief John Jennings the Testator in the pleadings of this Cause named was not at the time of his death possessed of or entitled unto or interested in any goods chattels household furniture plate linen china pictures books prints debts stock in the public funds monies on mortgage or other personal estate or effects other than and except such household furniture and effects as are by the said Testator specifically bequeathed to the said Defendant Alice Jennings and save and except such debts and such stocks in the public funds and monies on mortgage as are particularly set forth in the Schedule hereunder written marked with the letter A And this Defendant Midgley John Jennings further saith that he hath to the best of his knowledge in the said Schedule hereunder written (marked with the Letter A) set forth a full true and particular account of such debts stocks in the public funds monies on mortgage and other personal estate and effects of the said Testator John Jennings not specifically bequeathed got in received or possessed by this Defendant Midgley John Jennings or by any person by his order or for his use And this Defendant Midgley John Jennings further saith he hath in the said schedule hereunder written (marked with the Letter A) to the best of his knowledge set forth a full true and particular account of the personal estate and effects (not specifically bequeathed) of the said Testator John Jennings sold applied and disposed of since the decease of the said Testator John Jennings by this Defendant Midgley John Jennings or by any person or persons by his order or for his use And this Defendant Midgley John Jennings further saith that he hath in the said schedule hereunder written (marked with the Letter A) to the best of his knowledge and belief setforth a full true and particular account of such part of the said personal estate as consisted of sums of money due or owing to the said Testator John Jennings at the time of his decease and of the persons from whom the same were respectively due and owing and of the several securities given for the same and of the interest due on such of them as carried interest and of all sum and sums of money received by this Defendant Midgley John Jennings towards the payment of any debts owing to the Estate of the said John Jennings and that he this Defendant Midgley John Jennings hath in the said Schedule hereunder written (marked with the Letter A) to the best of his knowledge and belief set forth a full true and particular account of all sum and sums of money still remaining due in respect of such debts and of the interest thereof to the estate of the said Testator John Jennings the reasons why the same have not been gotten in And this Defendant Midgley John Jennings further saith that he hath to the best of his knowledge in the Schedule hereunder written (marked with the Letter B) set forth a full true and particular account of all and every sum and sums of money paid by this Defendant Midgley John Jennings or by any person or persons by his order or on his account in or towards payment of the debts of the said Testator or on account of the funeral expenses of the said Testator or otherwise on account of or incidental to his Estate or the Executorship thereof together with the names of the persons to whom and the purposes for which the same were so paid

Midgley John Jennings.   Jas. Trower

The Schedule A to which the above Examination refers

An Account of monies received by the Defendant Midgley John Jennings on account of the Estate of the Testator John Jennings

1805 April 3rd	Dividend or Interest on £2013.6.3. £5 per cents due October 1804	50.	6.	7.
	Of John Nattriss half a years interest on £150 due from him	4.	2.	6.
	Of Mr. Chappell in part of debt due from him	110.	0.	0.

6th	Of Mr. Potts for money advanced to him by the Testator	49.	17.	6.
	Of Mr. Rutledge Do	6.	10.	o.
June 18th	Dividend or Interest on £6493.6.0 £3 per cent consols due in January	97.	7.	11.
	Dividend or Interest on £2013.6.3.			
June 18th	£5 per cent due in April	50.	6.	7.
	Dividend on short annuities half a year	24.	o.	o.
July 6th	Dividend or Interest on £2307.10.0. £3 per cent reduced due in April	69.	4.	6.

July 25th | Half-year's Interest on £1200 mortgage on premises at Knightsbridge from the representatives of Hammond deceased due at Midsummer | 30. 0. 0.

19th   Dividend or Interest on £1000 East India
        Stock due in January   £52. 10. o. ⎫ 49. 17. 6.
        Income Tax deducted   2. 12. 6. ⎭

        The like due in July   £52. 10. o. ⎫ 49. 4. 5.
        Income tax deducted   3. 5. 7. ⎭

August 13th	Of Mr. Field amount of Bill due	4.	9.	o.
	Of Mr. Moorhouse—the like	8.	14.	6.
23rd	Of Mr. Hamilton—the like	3.	10.	o.
30th	Dividend or Interest on £6493.6.0. £3 pr. ct. consols due in July	97.	7.	11.

1805 April 1st	1/4 year's rent to Lady day 1805 of Swan and Hoop public house Moorgate a leasehold messuage belonging to the said Testator the Lease whereof expired at Lady day 1805.	11.	o.	o.
1805 April 6th	Of Mr. Rutt one years rent due at Lady day for a leasehold messuage adjoining the above the Lease whereof expired at Michaelmas last past	46.	o.	o.

An account of the funded property of the said
Testator John Jennings now standing in his name

   £1000 East India Stock
   £6493. 6. £3 per cent consolidated Bank annuities
   £2307. 10. £3 per cent reduced Bank annuities
   £2013. 6. 3. £5 per cent Bank annuities
   24   per annum short annuities

An account of the debts due to the Estate of the said
Testator still outstanding

£1200 from the Representatives of Hammond deceased
secured by Mortgage of premises at Knightsbridge
in Middlesex

150 from John Nattriss on security of a Deposit of
Title Deeds to Leasehold premises in Saint Georges
ffields & interest thereon from the 24th day
of July 1805

258.	6.	8.	from Mr. Chappell due from him residue of debt
16.	10.	0.	from Mr. Beckford whose affairs are in Chancery
46.	11.	6.	from Mr. Brenton on his note of hand very doubtful
11.	5.	0.	from Mr. Thompson doubtful
11.	14.	2.	from Mr. Lloyd
7.	14.	0.	from Mr. Nillock doubtful
3.	4.	0.	from Mr. Reed doubtful
9.	13.	6.	from Mr. Spottiswood doubtful
21.	16.	6.	from Mr. Taylor doubtful
23.	0.	0.	from Mr. Rutt, half years rent of house in pavement Moorfields—subject to Deductions for taxes
15.	0.	0.	from Mr. Pegram—or thereabouts the supposed Balance of an unsettled account.

Midgley John Jennings

The Schedule B to which the above examination refers

An Account of payments made by the Defendant Midgley John
Jennings on account of the Estate of the said Testator John Jennings

1805				
March 20th	Paid poors rate for house at Ponders End due at Xmas 1804	1.	17.	6.
March 25th	Pd chaise hire to London when attendg to prove will & coach-hire to Drs. Commons	1.	8.	0.
April 4th	Paid for a Book for accounts		2.	9.
	Paid Mr. Rawlings as per Bill	41.	4.	9.
	Pd. Registering Will in the £5 per cent office		2.	6.
	Paid for Probate of Will etc.	124.	18.	8.
	Paid Mr. Neyler as per Bill	12.	12.	6.
	Pd. Mr. Neal as per Bill		7.	10.
April 4th	Paid Mr. Knight the Minister	1.	1.	0.

June 25th	Paid Miss Fuller one years rent due 25th June	30.	0.	0.
	Paid Christian Finlayson servant her wages for 1 year to June 6th	7.	0.	0.
	Paid registering Will in reduced short Annuity and Consol offices at the Bank		12.	6.
	Pd Mr. Robinson Brandy Merchant	3.	15.	0.
July	Paid Messrs. Lowe & Co. Wine Merchants		18.	0.
6th	Paid Landlord's property tax on the Swan & Hoop Public House Moorgate due at Lady day	1.	8.	0.
	Pd. Do. on No. 22 Pavement Moorfields	1.	0.	0.
	Pd. Taxes on do. due 5th April	5.	7.	8.
	Pd. Mr. Hammond pr. his Bill	11.	17.	6.
25th	Pd. Rect. Stamp for Interest on £1200			8.
August	Pd. Mr. Camppen balance of accnt.	24.	4.	4.
7th	Pd. poors rates for house at Ponders End to Midsummer	1.	6.	0½
27th	Pd. for Servants mourning	2.	4.	7½
28th	Pd. taxes for house at Ponders End	7.	0.	2.
30th	Pd. property tax do	21.	15.	6.
	Pd. Mr. Hall the balance of his account	16.	12.	11.
Sept.	Retained half years annuity due 8th Sept.			
8th	to Deft. Midgley John Jennings	100.	0.	0.
	The like to Deft. Alice Jennings	100.	0.	0.
	The funeral expenses are unpaid no account thereof having been obtained	———		

This answer was taken and the above mentioned
Midgley John Jennings the Defendant was duly
sworn to the truth thereof on the Holy Evangelists
at the house of Edward Soan Twopenny at the Bishops
Precincts in the City of Rochester in the County of
Kent on the twenty eighth day of December in the year
of our Lord One thousand eight hundred and five by
virtue of the commission hereunto annexed before us

    E.S. Twopenny.   Edwd. Greenhill.

    Midgley John Jennings.

Prices of Stock held in trust for the Keats children under their grandmother's will

(Where no quotation was issued for the day, approximate prices are given.)

Date	3% Bank Consolidated annuities	3% Bank reduced annuities	5% stock
At date of Mrs. Jennings's will, July 31 1810	68¾	69⅜	99½
At approximate date of Mrs. Jennings's death in December 1814	66⅛	65½	97¼
At date of John Keats's coming-of-age, October 31 1816.	61⅞	60⅞	93⅞
At date of George Keats's coming-of-age, February 28 1818.	79⅛	79⅞	106¼
At approximate date of George's cashing his share, June 4 1818.	79⅛	78¼	108⅜
At date of Tom Keats's death, December 1 1818.	79	78¼	108⅝

At approximate date of George's return to cash Tom's share in January 1820	$67\frac{1}{4}$	$65\frac{3}{4}$	$103\frac{3}{8}$
At date of Fanny Keats's coming-of-age, June 3 1824.	$93\frac{7}{8}$	$94\frac{1}{4}$	$107\frac{7}{8}$[1]

[1] This quotation is for the new 4 per cent stock to which the 5 per cent stock had been converted.

John K. in account with Abbey Cock

Dr John K. in account with Abbey Cock.   C^r

1815				
June 9:—Sundries	1. —			
Decr. Tea. —	1			
1816. Sundries		1818		
Cocoa	10	June 4th By Cash—500		
Tea				
1817 do.		Decr. 31 Interest— 8–6.1		
do.	12			
do. &c		1819		
1818. Tea &c.—	X[2]	April 3^d.		
June 19:—Cash —	30			
20: do —	140			
July 9th —George Keats	30			
Aug. 8th Cash by Post	30			
Oct. 27. Cash —	20			
Decr. 9. Himself —	20			
1819. Febry 18: do. —	20			
Mar. 1 do. —	6			
„ 15th do. —	60			
„ 25 — do. —	10			
Aprl. 2 do. —	60			
Bal^{ce} — –	46—7—7			
	508—6 1.		508. 6. 1	

April 3^d. 1819 —

Accounts of money paid by Chancery to the Keats children

Frances Rawlings Life A/C

Order 13 Feb. 1810	Cash	Consols
Acnt Genl c.o.[1] from sd. cause being part of £2322.14.8. Consols		1666. 13. 4.
Order of 21 March 1823 paying to George Keats	416. 13. 4.	
Order of 3 June 1825 to Frances Mary Keats	416. 13. 4.	
Do Do	416. 13. 4.	
Do Do	416. 13. 4.	1666. 13. 4.

For the Divisions of
the Cash accrued on
above see next page

F.M. Keats here gets £1250

---

[1] Abbreviation for 'Accountant General, carried over'.

79

Frances Rawlings Life Account contd.

Cash

620

Order of 21st March 1823 Directs 1/4 of
the cash on the credit of cause to be
paid to George Keats

vizt £155

50
13
———
150
50
———
650

N.B. This £620 (i.e. with income tax it
would amount to £650?)[1] would take 13 years
accumulating thus showing that fund had not
been touched since death of Frances Rawlings

Order of 3 June 1825 pays to F.M. Keats 1/3rd of— 540
(which had increased to that amount from £465
during the above time.) vizt £180

620
155
———
465

Do   Do   (John Keats share)   180

Do   Do   (T. Keats share)   180

540.

---

[1] Ralph Thomas's query. The sum of £620 is in fact correct, representing the interest for 12 years and 4 months from the time the Accountant General actually purchased this stock, 8 months after Frances Rawlings's death.

Infant Legatees Account

(i.e. John George Thomas & Frances Mary Keats)

Consols

Order of 13th February 1810
Purchased by the Court of Chancery with Cash £1000   1550. 7. 10.
Mrs. Rawlings took interest for her life for
maintenance of her children by Report of 3 July
1811. She died February 1810.[1] The dividends on
the Fund then accumulated until Order of 21 March
1823 when it amounted to £
Order of 21 March 1823
paying to George Keats   387. 12. 0.
Order of 3 June 1825 to
Frances Mary Keats   387. 12. 0.
Do   do   do   (being
John Keats share)   387. 11. 11.
Order of 20 December 1825 ⎫
paying 1/3 of £387.11.11.   ⎪
of Thomas Keats share to   ⎬   387. 11. 11.
G. Keats   ⎪
Do   2/3 to F.M. Keats   ⎭   1550. 7. 10.

                    see next page
                              1550. 7. 10.
                               387. 11. 11.
                              ────────────
                              1162. 15. 11.

──

[1] Thomas here antedates her death by a month.

81

Order of 21 March 1823 that 1/4 of   534. 17. 10.
cash to credit of cause be paid to
George Keats
                    vizt. 133. 14. 5.
Order of 3 June 1825 transfers to
F. M. Keats one third of   470. 18. 9.
(N.B. The above sum of £534. 17. 10.
after deducting £133. 14. 5. had
increased to £470. 18. 9. during these
years)
                    vizt. 156. 19. 7.
Do   Do   J. Keats share
                    156. 19. 7.
This sum of £156. 19. 7. from date of
above Order to 20th December 1825 had
increased to £162. 15. 11.
Order of 20 December 1825 paying to
George Keats   £54. 5. 4.
being 1/3 of £162. 15. 11.
Order of same date paying to F.M. Keats
                    108. 10. 7.
                    —————————
being 2/3 of £162. 15. 11.   162. 15. 11.
                                    3
                               —————————

Family Tree
containing relatives of John Keats
connected with his grandfather's will
and subsequent Chancery suit

John Jennings = Alice Whalley
(? 1730–1805)   (1736–1814)

Frances = (1) Thomas Keats, (2) William Rawlings
(1775–   (?1774–1804)
1810)

JOHN KEATS   George   Thomas   Edward   Frances Mary
(1795–1821)   (1797–   (1799–   (1801–   (1803–1889)
              1842)   1818)   ?)

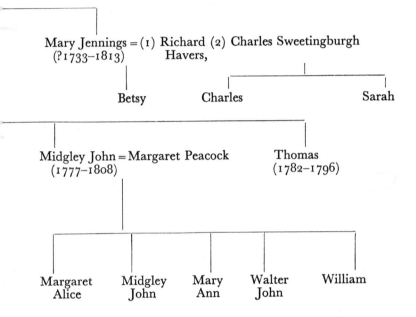

Mary Jennings = (1) Richard (2) Charles Sweetingburgh
(?1733–1813)   Havers,

Betsy   Charles   Sarah

Midgley John = Margaret Peacock   Thomas
(1777–1808)   (1782–1796)

Margaret   Midgley   Mary   Walter   William
Alice   John   Ann   John